# CHRISTMAS

# COOKBOOK

The Book Contains the Recipes You Need

(A Yummy Christmas Dessert Cookbook You Won't Be Able to Put Down)

**Edward Hogue**

Published by Alex Howard

© **Edward Hogue**

All Rights Reserved

*Christmas Cookbook: The Book Contains the Recipes You Need (A Yummy Christmas Dessert Cookbook You Won't Be Able to Put Down)*

**ISBN 978-1-989891-98-8**

All rights reserved. No part of this guide may be reproduced in any form without permission in writing from the publisher except in the case of brief quotations embodied in critical articles or reviews.

**Legal & Disclaimer**

The information contained in this book is not designed to replace or take the place of any form of medicine or professional medical advice. The information in this book has been provided for educational and entertainment purposes only.

The information contained in this book has been compiled from sources deemed reliable, and it is accurate to the best of the Author's knowledge; however, the Author cannot guarantee its accuracy and validity and cannot be held liable for any errors or omissions. Changes are periodically made to this book. You must consult your doctor or get professional medical advice before using any of the suggested remedies, techniques, or information in this book.

# Table of contents

**PART 1** .................................................................................................. 1

**CHAPTER 1 FABULOUS SPREADS & DIPS** ........................................... 2

    Christmas Eve Pecan Pimento Cheese Spread ............................................ 2
    Dancer's Delicious Chicken Spread ............................................................ 2
    Holly Jolly Ham Spread .............................................................................. 3
    Santa's Appetizing Crab Meat Spread ........................................................ 3
    Super Salmon Spread ................................................................................ 4
    Ambrosial Creamy Fruit Dip ...................................................................... 5
    Dasher's Favorite Parmesan Avocado Dip ................................................. 5
    Mrs. Claus's Supreme Shrimp Dip ............................................................. 6
    Spicy Bacon Blue Cheese Dip .................................................................... 6
    Whipped Chocolate Peppermint Dip ......................................................... 7

**CHAPTER 2 TASTY MEAT APPETIZERS AND SAVORY SAUCES** ........ 8

    Christmas Day Ham And Cheese Pinwheels .............................................. 8
    Delectable Glazed Meatballs .................................................................... 8
    Scrumptious Shrimp ................................................................................. 9
    Honey Lime Shrimp Sauce ....................................................................... 10
    Gourmet Salmon Puff Pastries ................................................................ 10
    Savory Sauces ........................................................................................ 11
    Blitzen's Spicy Horseradish Sauce ........................................................... 11
    Elves Blue Cheese Dipping Sauce ............................................................ 12
    Magnificent Chipotle Cranberry Sauce .................................................... 12

**CHAPTER 3 HOLIDAY BUTTERS AND BREADS** ................................ 14

    Cinnamon Honey Butter ......................................................................... 14
    Frosty's Honey Pecan Butter ................................................................... 14
    Heavenly Lemon Butter .......................................................................... 14
    Luscious Cranberry Orange Sauce Butter ................................................ 15
    Pecan Pumpkin Spice Streusel Muffins ................................................... 15
    Dreamy Brown Sugar Streusel ................................................................ 16
    Rudolph's Chocolate Chip Walnut Bread ................................................ 17
    Sweet Cherry Eggnog Bread ................................................................... 18
    White Christmas Cinnamon Rolls ............................................................ 18

## CHAPTER 4 CELEBRATION CHEESEBALLS ........................................................... 20

DECK THE HALLS SPICY JALAPENO CHEESEBALL ....................................................... 20
HOLIDAY CHEESEBALL TRIO ........................................................................................ 20
SNOWFLAKES COCONUT CHEESEBALL ........................................................................ 21
SPRINKLED COOKIE DOUGH CHIP CHEESEBALL .......................................................... 22

## CHAPTER 5 DIVINE DESSERTS & DECADENT SAUCES ................................. 23

CANDY CANE OREO TRUFFLES .................................................................................... 23
EGGNOG BROWNIE BITES ICE CREAM ........................................................................ 23
MINI WHIPPED CHOCOLATE CHIP CHEESECAKES ....................................................... 24
SUGAR AND SPICE GINGERBREAD CUPCAKES ............................................................ 25
DECADENT SAUCES ..................................................................................................... 26
COMET'S CARAMEL SAUCE ......................................................................................... 26
CUPID'S CHOCOLATE FUDGE SAUCE .......................................................................... 26
WHITE CHOCOLATE SAUCE ......................................................................................... 27

## CHAPTER 6 NUTCRACKER SNACK MIXES ......................................................... 28

CHRISTMAS CINNAMON MIXED PARTY NUTS ............................................................ 28
CITRUS HONEY CASHEWS ........................................................................................... 28
FESTIVE WHITE CHOCOLATE POPCORN ..................................................................... 29
GINGERED ORANGE ALMONDS .................................................................................. 30
HOLIDAY SPICED PECANS ............................................................................................ 30
NOEL CRANBERRY CHEX MIX ...................................................................................... 31
CHRISTMAS RECIPES .................................................................................................... 33
(1) WHITE CHRISTMAS ROCKY ROAD ........................................................................ 33
(2) SPARKLING SUGAR PLUMS .................................................................................... 34
(3) HOMEMADE HAZELNUT AND CHOCOLATE SPREAD ........................................... 37
(4) BACON AND CARAMELIZED ONION JAM .............................................................. 39
(5) VANILLA GRAPEFRUIT SHORTBREAD ................................................................... 41
(6) BOOZY CHRISTMAS CUPCAKES ............................................................................. 42
(7) TEACHER'S TREAT ................................................................................................... 45
(8) BRANDIED FRUIT ..................................................................................................... 47
(9) SNOWBALL TRUFFLES ............................................................................................ 48
(10) CABERNET CRANBERRY AND BLUEBERRY SAUCE .............................................. 51
(11) SILVER STAR GINGER COOKIES ........................................................................... 53
(12) CANDY CANE CHOCOLATE FUDGE ..................................................................... 55

(13) SILVER AND GOLD DUST DATE TRUFFLES .................................................. 56
(14) CHERRY ESPRESSO BISCOTTI ........................................................................ 58
(15) PUMPKIN SPICE WHIPPED HONEY BUTTER ................................................ 59
(16) CHOCOLATE COATED CHERRIES ................................................................... 60
(17) PIXIE DUSTED WHITE CHOCOLATE ALMONDS ......................................... 62
(18) CHOCOLATE DIPPED LICORICE ...................................................................... 63
(19) PEPPERMINT CRACKER TOFFEE .................................................................... 65
(20) CHOCOLATE PEPPERMINT SPOONS ............................................................. 66
(21) PASSIONFRUIT CARAMELS ............................................................................. 67
(22) CINNAMON SPICED CANDIED PECANS ....................................................... 69
(23) NONNA'S HOMEMADE LIMONCELLO .......................................................... 70
(24) CLEMENTINE CHRISTMAS CURD ................................................................... 71
(25) MULLED WINE KIT ............................................................................................ 73
(26) COCONUT LIME SNOWBALLS ........................................................................ 75
(27) MINI BRIE AND JAM PIE .................................................................................. 76
(28) ESPRESSO SUGAR CUBES ............................................................................... 78
(29) MINCE PIE COOKIES ......................................................................................... 80
(30) FRUITY JELLIES .................................................................................................. 81
(31) MEXICAN SPICED HOT COCOA JAR MIX .................................................... 84
(32) GLITTER POPS .................................................................................................... 86
(33) MERRY MUFFIN MIX IN A JAR ...................................................................... 88
(34) GLITTERY STRAWBERRY JAM WITH PROSECCO ...................................... 90
(35) MARINATED FETA CHEESE ............................................................................. 92
(36) GOLDEN CHILLI VODKA .................................................................................. 94
(37) HOMEMADE VANILLA EXTRACT ................................................................... 95
(38) HIBISCUS HOME INFUSED VODKA ............................................................... 97
(39) HOMEMADE HERBY SALT ............................................................................... 98
(40) HOLLY COOKIES ................................................................................................ 99

## PART 2 ................................................................................................................... 101

## INTRODUCTION ..................................................................................................... 102

SUGAR CUT OUT COOKIES ...................................................................................... 103
BUTTER CUT OUT COOKIES .................................................................................... 105
CHOCOLATE CUT OUT COOKIES ............................................................................ 107
GINGERBREAD CUT OUT COOKIES ....................................................................... 109
SOFT CUT OUT COOKIES ......................................................................................... 111

- Cream Cheese Cut Out Cookies .................................................................... 113
- Shortbread Cut Out Cookies ........................................................................ 114
- Anise Cut Out CookiesIngredients ............................................................. 115
- Vanilla Cut Out Cookies ............................................................................... 117
- Chocolate Spice Cut Out Cookies ................................................................. 119
- Almond Shortbread Cut Out Cookies .......................................................... 121
- Chocolate Shortbread Cookies ..................................................................... 123
- Apple Cinnamon Cut Out Cookies ............................................................... 125
- Simple Scottish Shortbread Cut Out Cookies ............................................. 127
- German Cut Out Cookies .............................................................................. 128
- Pumpkin Cut Out Cookies ............................................................................. 130
- Cinnamon Cut Out Cookies .......................................................................... 132
- Sour Cream Cut Out Cookies ........................................................................ 134
- Crispy Cornmeal Cut Out Cookies ................................................................ 136
- Brown Sugar Shortbread Cookies ................................................................ 138
- Oat Flour Cut Out Cookies ............................................................................ 139
- Whole Wheat Cut Out Cookies ..................................................................... 141
- Soft Gingerbread Cookies ............................................................................. 142
- Pumpkin Gingerbread Cut Out Cookies ...................................................... 144
- Chocolate Brownie Cut Out Cookies ........................................................... 146
- Chocolate Cherry Cut Out Cookies .............................................................. 148
- Dark Chocolate Cut Out Sugar Cookies ....................................................... 150
- Orange Chocolate Cut Out Cookies ............................................................. 152
- White Chocolate Cut Out Cookies ............................................................... 154
- Molasses Cut Out Cookies ............................................................................ 156
- Orange Cut Out Sugar Cookies .................................................................... 158
- Orange Butter Cut Out Cookies ................................................................... 160
- Chocolate Raspberry Cut Out Cookies ........................................................ 162
- Ginger Spice Cut Out Cookies ...................................................................... 164
- Chocolate Coconut Cut Out Cookies ........................................................... 166
- Lemon Shortbread Cut Out Cookies ............................................................ 168
- Banana Cut Out Cookies ............................................................................... 170
- Mint Chocolate Cut Out Cookies .................................................................. 172
- Cranberry Cut Out Sugar Cookies ................................................................ 174
- Eggnog Cut Out Cookies ............................................................................... 176
- Cinnamon Mint Cut Out Cookies ................................................................. 178

RED VELVET CUT OUT COOKIES ..................................................................... 180
MOCHA CUT OUT COOKIES............................................................................. 182
CHOCOLATE PEANUT BUTTER CUT OUT COOKIES.................................................. 184
TOFFEE CUT OUT COOKIES ............................................................................ 186
CHOCOLATE CARAMEL CUT OUT COOKIES ......................................................... 187

# Part 1

# Chapter 1 Fabulous Spreads & Dips

## Christmas Eve Pecan Pimento Cheese Spread

1/2 cup pecans

1/2 cup pimiento stuffed Spanish olives, chopped

3/4 cup mayonnaise

1/3 cup bottled chili sauce

1 tsp. Worcestershire sauce

10 oz. block finely shredded sharp cheddar cheese

Toast pecans for 8 minutes in a single layer in a preheated oven at 350 degrees. Let cool, then finely chop them into pieces. In a bowl, add mayonnaise, olives, chili sauce, and Worcestershire sauce, and blend well. Mix in cheese and pecans till smooth. Serve with vegetables (celery, carrot sticks, radishes), and crackers. Makes 8 servings.

## Dancer's Delicious Chicken Spread

2 cups chopped cooked chicken

16 oz. Cream cheese softened

6 tbs. Chutney

4 finely chopped green onions

4 tbs. Mayonnaise

3 tsp. Curry powder

Garnish: Finely chopped walnuts

In a food processor, grind chicken, chutney and onions. In a bowl, beat cream cheese, mayonnaise, and curry till light and fluffy. Fold this into chicken mixture. Top with walnuts, and serve with holiday breads. Makes 4 1/2 cups.

## Holly Jolly Ham Spread

6 cups ground cooked ham

4 tsp. Sweet pickle relish

3 chopped hard boiled eggs

4 tbs. Finely chopped celery

4 tsp. Finely chopped onion

1 1/2 cups mayonnaise

2 tbs. Prepared mustard

Garnish: Finely chopped fresh parsley

In a bowl, combine all ingredients except the mayonnaise and the mustard. In a small bowl, mix mayonnaise and mustard, then add to the ham mixture, blend well. Keep refrigerated till serving, and top with finely chopped fresh parsley. Serve with an assortment of crackers. Makes 6 cups.

## Santa's Appetizing Crab Meat Spread

4 oz. Real lump crab meat

1/8 cup diced red pepper

1/8 cup diced red onion

1 tbs. Mayonnaise

1 tbs. Sour cream

Salt and pepper to taste

1/2 tsp. Lemon juice

Garnish: Finely chopped chives

Separate lump crab meat into pieces, and add in remaining ingredients. Combine well together. Transfer to a serving bowl and garnish with chives on top. Makes 12 servings.

## Super Salmon Spread

8 oz. Cold smoked salmon, broken into pieces

1/2 cup sour cream

12 oz. Cream cheese softened

2 tbs. Finely diced red onion

1 tbs. Fresh lemon juice

1 tbs. Drained capers

1 tbs. Chopped fresh dill

Dash of salt and ground black pepper

In a food processor, mix cream cheese, salmon, 1/2 of the red onion, lemon juice, sour cream, capers, and 1/2 of the dill and pepper. Blend till a coarse puree forms. Season with salt. Transfer spread mixture to a serving bowl, and sprinkle with remaining onion and dill. Serve with bagel chips. Makes 3 cups.

# Ambrosial Creamy Fruit Dip

1/2 cup red raspberry preserves

6 oz. Package cream cheese softened

1 cup sour cream

2 tsp. Finely shredded lemon peel

2 tbs. Lemon juice

Garnish: Fresh Fruit Dippers

In a bowl, beat the cream cheese till light and fluffy. Stir in the sour cream, preserves, lemon peel, and juice till blended. Using cocktail picks, spear the fruit ( apple wedges, strawberries, cherries, pineapple chunks) and place in the dip. Makes 2 cups.

# Dasher's Favorite Parmesan Avocado Dip

2 large avocados, peeled and seeded

4 slices cooked crumbled bacon, drained

1 cup sour cream

1/2 cup grated Parmesan cheese

2 tbs. Lemon juice

Salt to taste

In a mixing bowl, mash the avocado, and add in the sour cream, cheese, lemon juice, and the salt. Transfer to a serving bowl. Cover and refrigerate for 2 hours. Garnish with crumbled bacon, and serve with vegetable dippers such as cauliflower or broccoli florets, and green pepper rings, and assorted crackers. Makes 2 1/2 cups.

## Mrs. Claus's Supreme Shrimp Dip

9 oz. Can shrimp, chopped and drained

3 cups sour cream

2 chopped hard boiled eggs

6 tbs. Sliced green onion

4 tbs. Milk

2 tbs. Lemon juice

2 tsp. Worcestershire sauce

1 tsp. Dried dill weed

In a bowl, mix sour cream, shrimp, onion, eggs, lemon juice, milk, Worcestershire sauce, and dill, till combined well. Cover and refrigerate. Add additional milk if needed. Serve with vegetables. Makes 4 cups.

## Spicy Bacon Blue Cheese Dip

4 cooked bacon slices, crumbled

1/2 cup sour cream

4 oz. Package crumbled blue cheese

3 oz. Package cream cheese softened

2 tbs. Diced onion

1/4 tsp. Hot sauce

In a food processor, blend all ingredients, except for bacon till smooth. Then, stir in 1/2 of the bacon pieces. Cover and refrigerate for 2 hours. Sprinkle remaining crumbled bacon on dip before serving at room temperature. Serve with assorted crackers. Makes 1 1/2 cups.

## Whipped Chocolate Peppermint Dip

1/4 cup mini peppermint crushed sticks
1/3 cup chocolate chips
4 oz. Cream cheese
1 container frozen whipped topping

With an electric mixer, beat the cream cheese till fluffy, and whisk in the whipped topping. Add in the crushed peppermint sticks, and stir in the chocolate chips. Serve with graham crackers or vanilla wafers, or Oreo cookies. Makes 8 servings.

# Chapter 2 Tasty Meat Appetizers And Savory Sauces

## Christmas Day Ham And Cheese Pinwheels

2 roll tubes of crescent dough sheets

24 thin slices Swiss cheese

1 1/2 lbs. Thin sliced black forest ham

2 tbs. Poppy seeds

1 cup melted salted butter

3 tbs. yellow mustard

2 tbs. Dried minced onion

1 tsp. Worcestershire sauce

Preheat oven to 350 degrees, and spray with cooking spray 2(9x13 inch) baking dishes. Roll out each crescent roll dough into a 13x18 inch rectangle. Top each dough sheet with ham and cheese. Beginning with the long side roll up the dough tightly, pinching the ends together, placing them with the seam facing down. Slice each roll into 12 pieces each. Place 12 pinwheels in each baking dish, allowing space between each of them. In a bowl, combine the butter, poppy seeds, mustard, onion, and Worcestershire sauce. Spoon this sauce mixture over each pinwheel. Bake uncovered for 20-25 minutes until browned. Makes 24 pinwheels.

## Delectable Glazed Meatballs

1 lb. Ground beef

1/4 cup ketchup

1/2 tbs. Prepared horseradish

1 1/2 slices bread

1/4 cup milk

1 lightly beaten egg

1/8 cup maple flavored syrup

1/8 cup water

1/8 cup soy sauce

1/2 tsp. Ground allspice

1/4 tsp. Dry mustard

Salt and pepper to taste

In a bowl, soak bread in milk till it is a soft texture. Stir in egg, horseradish, salt and pepper and mix till smooth. Add in the beef, and combine well. Shape into 1/2 inch meatballs, and place on the rack in a shallow baking pan. Bake in oven at 450 degrees for 15-20 minutes. In a saucepan, heat the remaining ingredients to a boil, stirring consistently. Remove meatballs from the oven, take tongs and place them in the saucepan, heating them through, simmering on low. Serve them on wooden picks. Makes 32 meatballs.

## Scrumptious Shrimp

3 lbs. raw shrimp peeled and deveined

6 cups Panko bread crumbs

6 tbs. Olive oil

Dash of Kosher salt

3 tsp. Garlic powder

Ground black pepper to taste

6 large eggs

3 cups all purpose flour

Garnish: Finely chopped fresh cilantro

Preheat the oven to 400 degrees and line a baking sheet with parchment paper. In a mixing bowl, combine oil, breadcrumbs, and garlic powder. Sprinkle with salt and pepper to season. In a separate bowl, whisk the eggs together. In a third bowl, add flour. Using a pair of tongs, dip the shrimp first in the flour, secondly in the egg bowl, and third in the Panko mixture. Transfer each one to the baking sheet fully coated. Bake for 15 minutes till crispy and golden brown. Drizzle honey lime sauce over each shrimp, and garnish with cilantro. Makes 12 servings.

## Honey Lime Shrimp Sauce

3 tsp. Honey

Juice from 3 limes

3 tbs. Sriracha

Kosher salt to taste

6 tbs. Sweet chili sauce

6 tbs. Mayonnaise

In a mixing bowl, whisk the mayonnaise, sriracha, chili sauce, lime juice, honey, and season with the kosher salt.

## Gourmet Salmon Puff Pastries

15 1/2 oz. Canned salmon

16 oz. Package phyllo dough

1 1/2 cups melted butter

4 beaten eggs

2 cups cottage cheese(creamy), drained

1 cup finely chopped cucumber

2 tsp. Dried dill weed

1 tsp. Lemon pepper

Drain the salmon from the can, flake it, removing the bones and skin. Mix with the eggs, cheese, dill weed, cucumber, and lemon pepper. Unfolding the phyllo dough, spread one sheet flat, brushing with butter. Top this with a second sheet, brush with butter, and then top with a third sheet, brushing with butter. Slice stack of sheets lengthwise into 2 inch strips. Place 1 tbs. of the salmon mixture at the end of each strip. Fold the end over the filling, to form a triangle. The triangle should enclose the filling, using the complete strip of three layers. Repeat the process with the remaining dough and filling. Place them on the baking sheet, and brush with butter. Bake at 375 degrees for 20 minutes in the oven. Serve immediately. Makes 64 servings.

## Savory Sauces

## Blitzen's Spicy Horseradish Sauce

1 1/2 tsp. Horseradish

1 tsp. Dijon mustard

1/4 cup sour cream

Garnish: Cilantro

Blend together all ingredients in a mixing bowl. Cover and chill at least 3 1/2 hours. Makes 1/4 cup. Perfect for prime rib, sirloin steak, and filet mignon.

## Elves Blue Cheese Dipping Sauce

Hot pepper sauce to taste
2 tbs. Crumbled blue cheese
2 tbs. Mayonnaise
1/4 cup sour cream
1 tsp. Red wine vinegar
1 tsp. Fresh lemon juice

In a bowl, whisk the blue cheese, mayonnaise, sour cream, vinegar, lemon juice, and hot pepper sauce together. Transfer to serving bowl. Makes 1/2 cup. Serve with buffalo chicken wings.

## Magnificent Chipotle Cranberry Sauce

1 canned Chipotle pepper in adobo sauce, minced
1 cup whole berry cranberry sauce
1/3 cup taco sauce
1 tsp. Chili powder
Dash of salt
1/2 tsp. Ground cumin

In a microwave safe bowl, place all ingredients except for the salt. Microwave on high for 2 minutes, or until a thick mixture forms, stirring after 1 minute. Season with salt to taste. Makes 1 1/3 cups. This rich sauce is great with turkey and ham.

# Chapter 3 Holiday Butters And Breads

## Cinnamon Honey Butter

2 tsp. Cinnamon

2 tbs. Honey

1/4 cup brown sugar

1 cup softened butter

Combine all the ingredients into a bowl, and refrigerate in an airtight container for at least 15 minutes. Serve with ham, or breads. Makes 16 servings.

## Frosty's Honey Pecan Butter

1 tbs. Honey

1/3 cup toasted finely chopped pecans

1/2 cup softened butter

1 tsp. Chopped fresh rosemary

In a mixing bowl, stir all ingredients together.Cover and store in refrigerator. Serve butter at room temperature with breads. Makes 3/4 cup serving.

## Heavenly Lemon Butter

2 tsp. Lemon zest

Salt and pepper to taste

1/3 cup dry white wine

1 tbs. White wine vinegar

1/4 cup minced shallots

3/4 cup softened butter

1 tbs. Chopped fresh tarragon

In a saucepan, add wine, vinegar, and shallots. Cook on medium for 5 minutes, till liquid is reduced. Remove pan from heat, and let cool for 10 minutes. Mix in the butter and all other ingredients. Store mixture in an airtight container, and refrigerate. Serve with turkey. Makes 1 cup.

## Luscious Cranberry Orange Sauce Butter

12 tbs. Whole berry cranberry sauce

8 tsp. Orange marmalade

2 sticks unsalted softened butter

4 tsp. Confectioners's sugar

Dash of salt

In a food processor, process all ingredients until well blended. Place in an airtight container, and store in refrigerator. Serve with breads. Makes 28 servings.

## Pecan Pumpkin Spice Streusel Muffins

3/4 cup canned pumpkin

1/4 cup toasted chopped pecans

1/2 cup softened butter

4 oz. Package softened cream cheese

1/2 cup granulated sugar

1/2 cup light brown sugar

1 large egg

1 1/2 cups all purpose flour

1/2 tsp. Pumpkin pie spice

1/4 tsp. Baking powder

1/4 tsp. Baking soda

Salt to taste

1/4 cup sweetened dried cranberries

1/4 tsp. Vanilla extract

Preheat the oven to 350 degrees. Mix the butter and cream cheese in an electric stand mixer on medium till mixture is creamy. Add in the sugars, combining till fluffy. Add the egg, and blend well. In a mixing bowl, stir the flour, spice, baking powder, baking soda, and salt. Add this mixture to the butter mixture, beating it on low speed. Add in the pumpkin, pecans, cranberries, and extract. Spray a 12 cup muffin pan with cooking spray, and spoon the batter into the muffin pan, filling each cup 2/3 full. Sprinkle the streusel over each of them. Bake at 350 degrees for 20-25 minutes, or until the wooden toothpick inserted comes out clean. Cool in the pans for 15 minutes. Remove from pan to wire racks to completely cool for 15 more minutes. Makes 12 muffins.

## Dreamy Brown Sugar Streusel

1/4 tsp. Pumpkin pie spice

1/4 cup chopped pecans

1/4 cup light brown sugar

1/2 tbs. all purpose flour

1/2 tbs. Melted butter

Combine brown sugar, pecans, butter, flour, and the spice till well blended, in a mixing bowl.

## Rudolph's Chocolate Chip Walnut Bread

1/4 cup semisweet chocolate chips

1/4 cup chopped walnuts

1 1/4 cups all purpose flour

3/4 cup sugar

1/2 tbs. Baking powder

1/4 cup vegetable shortening

2 eggs

1/2 cup cranberry juice cocktail

1/8 cup chocolate flavored syrup

1/2 cup dried cranberries

Preheat the oven to 350 degrees, and spray with cooking spray a 4x8 inch loaf pan. In a bowl, stir the flour, sugar, and baking powder. Use an electric mixer to beat in the shortening till combined. Add in the eggs, chocolate syrup, and cranberry juice till well blended. Fold in the chocolate chips, walnuts, and the cranberries. Pour the batter into the prepared loaf pan. Bake for 50-55 minutes or until the wooden toothpick inserted in the center comes out clean. Cool 15 minutes before removing from pan, transfer to wire rack to cool completely for 20 minutes more. Makes 1 bread loaf.

## Sweet Cherry Eggnog Bread

1/2 cup chopped maraschino cherries

2/3 cup refrigerated eggnog

1/4 cup chopped walnuts

1/4 cup canola oil

Salt to taste

1 1/4 cups all purpose flour

1/2 cup sugar

1 beaten egg

1/2 tbs. Baking powder

Preheat the oven to 350 degrees, and spray with cooking spray a 8x4x2 inch loaf pan. In a bowl, combine the baking powder, salt, sugar, and flour. Add in the eggnog and the oil. Stir the dry ingredients into the wet ingredients, and blend well. Fold in the walnuts, and the cherries into the mixture. Pour the batter into the loaf pan, and bake 40-45 minutes, or until toothpick inserted in center comes out clean. Makes 1 bread loaf.

## White Christmas Cinnamon Rolls

1 tsp. Ground cinnamon

1/4 cup sifted confectioners's sugar

1/4 cup heavy whipping cream

1/2 tsp. Water

1/2 lb. Loaf frozen bread dough, thawed

1 1/2 tbs. Melted butter

1/4 cup brown sugar

1/4 cup finely chopped walnuts

1 tbs. Milk

Dash of vanilla extract

Spray a round cake pan with cooking spray. Roll the bread dough out with rolling pin into a 6x18 inch rectangle. Brush over it with melted butter. In a bowl, stir in the walnuts, cinnamon, and brown sugar, and sprinkle the mixture over the buttered dough. Roll the dough up into a log, beginning at the long edge. Moisten the edge with the water to seal. Slice the log into 10 slices, arranging the rolls cut sides down, in the cake pan. Cover with a towel to let it rise in a warm environment until it is doubled in volume for 90 minutes. Preheat the oven to 350 degrees. Pour the heavy cream over the dough rolls. Bake for 20-25 minutes until lightly browned. In a bowl, stir the confectioners's sugar, extract, and milk together. Remove rolls from oven and drizzle this glaze over the warm rolls. Makes 10 servings.

# Chapter 4 Celebration Cheeseballs

## Deck The Halls Spicy Jalapeno Cheeseball

2/3 cup finely diced jalapeno pepper(seeds and stem removed)
3 finely minced cloves
1 cup natural sliced almonds
1 cup chopped walnuts
2/3 cup cooked crumbled bacon
1 cup finely diced red bell pepper(seeds and stem removed)
2/3 cup finely diced red onion
24 oz. Brick style cream cheese softened
16 oz. Grated sharp cheddar cheese

In a bowl, mix all the ingredients together except for the nuts. Combine by stirring by hand, or use an electric mixer on low speed. Roll mixture into a ball. Wrap in plastic wrap, and refrigerate for 3 hours to chill and set. Transfer ball to serving platter, and cover with the walnuts and almonds. Roll the ball in the nuts till completely covered. Makes 24 servings.

## Holiday Cheeseball Trio

32 oz. Softened cream cheese
1 lb. Shredded cheddar cheese
1/4 cup evaporated milk
1 cup finely chopped pecans

2 1/4 oz. Finely chopped ripe olives, drained

Dash of salt

2 minced garlic cloves

Garnish: Paprika, chopped pecans, minced fresh parsley

In a bowl, stir cream cheese, cheddar cheese, pecans, garlic, salt, and olives. Divide the mixture into thirds, and roll each one of them into a ball. Roll one in the paprika, the parsley,and the nuts. Cover and refrigerate each cheeseball, for 3 hours. Remove from refrigerator 15 minutes prior to serving with assorted crackers. Makes 3 cheeseballs.

## Snowflakes Coconut Cheeseball

1/4 lb. Finely chopped ham

2 cups toasted coconut

18 oz. Brick cream cheese, softened

1 cup Monterey Jack cheese

1/2 cup sour cream

1/2 cup pineapple

In a mixing bowl, combine cream cheese, sour cream, cheese, pineapple, and ham. Mold cheese mixture into a ball. Wrap in plastic wrap and chill for 2 hours. Sprinkle the toasted coconut on the serving platter, remove cheeseball from refrigerator, and roll the cheeseball in the coconut. Serve with rice crackers. Makes one cheeseball.

# Sprinkled Cookie Dough Chip Cheeseball

2 cups mini chocolate chips

1 1/2 cups multicolored sprinkles

16 oz. Cream cheese softened

1 stick softened butter

1 cup powdered sugar

1/2 cup brown sugar

1 tsp. Vanilla extract

In a mixing bowl, use a hand mixer, and combine the butter and cream cheese until fluffy. Add in the powdered sugar, vanilla, brown sugar, and fold in the chocolate chips. Roll into a ball, place in a bowl, cover with plastic wrap, refrigerate till firm, around 3 1/2 hours. Transfer ball to serving plate, cover it with sprinkles, and roll the cheeseball in it, till thoroughly coated. Serve with vanilla wafers. Makes 20 servings.

# Chapter 5 Divine Desserts & Decadent Sauces

## Candy Cane Oreo Truffles

20 regular Oreo cookies

1/2 tsp. Peppermint extract

8 oz. Semisweet chocolate finely chopped

1 regular size crushed candy cane

1/2 tbs. Coconut oil

4 oz. Softened cream cheese

In food processor, place the cookies, and pulse till ground completely. Mix in the cream cheese and the peppermint extract, pulsing till smooth. With parchment paper, line a rimmed baking sheet. Scoop this mixture into 18 individual balls, and place in freezer for 2 hours till chilled and set. In a microwave safe bowl, stir chocolate and oil together, microwaving at 20 second intervals till melted completely. Remove the balls from the freezer, dropping them in the melted chocolate mixture, coating them thoroughly. Place on a cookie sheet and sprinkle each one with crushed candy cane pieces. Refrigerate for 1 1/2 hours till set before transferring to serving plate. Makes 18 truffles.

## Eggnog Brownie Bites Ice Cream

2 boxes brownie mixes(follow ingredients required)

3 cups refrigerated eggnog

3 cups heavy cream

Dash ground nutmeg

1 1/2 cups sugar

Prepare the brownies according to directions and ingredients in 2 (8x8inch pans). Let them cool for 20 minutes till set. In a bowl, mix together the cream and sugar until completely dissolved. Stir in the eggnog and the nutmeg till blended. Place the eggnog mixture into a ice cream maker and process according to its directions, creating a soft serve consistency. Pour this soft ice cream back into a bowl. Slice 1/2 of the brownies into small chunks and place into the ice cream. Pour this ice cream mixture into the pans lined with parchment paper. Freeze for 3 hours. Remove from freezer, scoop ice cream out and place in parfait glasses, and garnish on top with remaining brownie chunks. Makes 12 servings.

## Mini Whipped Chocolate Chip Cheesecakes

1 package ready to bake chocolate chip cookies

3 cups Reddi-wip cream topping

1 cup semisweet chocolate chips

16 oz. Softened cream cheese

1 cup sugar

2 tbs. Coconut oil

Preheat oven to 350 degrees, and spray with cooking spray 2 (12 cup) muffin tins. Place one chocolate chip dough square in each of the 24 cups. Bake for 12-15 minutes, and cool 20 minutes. In a mixing bowl, blend cream cheese and sugar with an electric mixer on medium speed till smooth. Spoon this topping over cheesecakes with 1/2 of the Reddi-wip until each cup is filled, and with a spatula smooth top till flat. Freeze 3 1/2 hours to set. In a microwave safe bowl, place chocolate chips and oil, and microwave at 20 second intervals till the chocolate is melted, and whisk till mixture is smooth. Remove the muffin tins from the freezer. Release the cheesecakes from the cups. Place on the cooling racks, and drizzle the chocolate mixture over each one. Let them stand at room temperature for 15 minutes. Squirt remaining Reddi-wip on top of each mini cheesecake. Makes 24 servings.

## Sugar And Spice Gingerbread Cupcakes

3/4 cup all purpose flour

1/2 cup whole wheat flour

1 1/4 tsp. Baking soda

1/2 cup unsweetened applesauce

1/2 cup molasses

1/2 tsp. Ground ginger

1/2 tsp. Ground cinnamon

1/2 tsp. Ground allspice

1/2 cup sugar

1/4 cup canola oil

1 egg white

1 egg

1/4 tsp. Salt

1 cup whipped topping

In a bowl, combine the egg white, egg, sugar, and oil till well blended. Mix in the applesauce and molasses stirring well. In a separate bowl, combine the flours, ginger, baking soda, allspice, cinnamon, and salt. Add these to the applesauce mixture till blended and smooth. Fill a 12 cup muffin pan with baking paper cups, and spoon 2/3 full of the batter mixture. Bake in a 350 degree oven for 20-25 minutes or until toothpick inserted in center comes out clean. Cool 20 minutes before removing from pan to a wire rack. Let cool completely an additional 15 minutes. Place whipped topping on each cupcake before serving. Makes 12 small cupcakes or 10 large cupcakes.

# Decadent Sauces

## Comet's Caramel Sauce

1 1/4 cups brown sugar

1/4 cup butter

1 cup light corn syrup

1 cup whipping heavy cream

1 cup finely chopped toasted pecans

In a saucepan, heat brown sugar, butter, and corn syrup to boiling, quickly reduce to low heat, stirring frequently. Boil again, stirring consistently, then stir in whipping cream, bringing to a boil. Let simmer, then cool for 30 minutes. Makes 2 1/2 cups. Serve with pound cake.

## Cupid's Chocolate Fudge Sauce

12 oz. Semisweet chocolate chips

1/2 cup sugar

1 tsp. Vanilla extract
1 tbs. Butter
12 oz. Evaporated milk

In a 2 qt. Saucepan, place chocolate chips, sugar, and milk, heating to a boil, while stirring constantly. Remove from heat, and add butter and vanilla extract. Blend till smooth and creamy. Makes 3 cups. Serve with ice cream, truffles, cheesecakes.

## White Chocolate Sauce

12 oz. White vanilla baking chips
1/4 tsp. Almond extract
2 tbs. Butter
1 cup slivered almonds
1 cup whipping heavy cream

In a large saucepan, heat on medium, the almonds and butter for 8 minutes, stirring till brown. Remove from the heat, and stir in the whipping cream, blending well. Add in the baking chips and heat on low till they are melted. Then, stir in the extract. Makes 2 3/4 cups. Serve with fruit or cakes.

# Chapter 6 Nutcracker Snack Mixes

## Christmas Cinnamon Mixed Party Nuts

11.5 oz. Salted mixed nuts

1/4 tsp. Ground cinnamon

1 tbs. Melted butter

2 tsp. Chili powder

1/2 tsp. Garlic powder

1/2 tsp. Onion powder

2 tbs. Sugar

1/4 tsp. Ground red cayenne pepper

Preheat the oven to 300 degrees. In a mixing bowl, stir the nuts and butter till well coated. In a separate bowl, combine the remaining ingredients except for the sugar. Sprinkle this mixture over the nut mixture till blended. Spray a baking sheet with cooking spray and place the mixture uncovered in a single layer for 10 minutes. Transfer to a serving bowl, while they are still warm, sprinkle the sugar on them. Let cool completely for one hour, then store in an airtight container. Makes 9 servings.

## Citrus Honey Cashews

4 cups cashews

2 tbs. Honey

1/4 cup butter

1 tbs. Orange zest

1 tbs. Finely chopped fresh rosemary

Kosher salt to taste

Preheat the oven to 350 degrees. In a saucepan cook the butter on medium a few minutes till it turns lightly brown. Remove the pan from the heat, and add in cashews, honey, and orange zest. On a rimmed baking sheet lined with parchment paper, pour the cashew mixture in a single layer. Season with salt. Bake for 10 minutes at 350 degrees, till roasted, stirring halfway through. Sprinkle on the rosemary. Bake an additional few minutes till fragrant. Remove from oven and let cool completely for 30 minutes, then store in an airtight container. Makes 4 cups.

## Festive White Chocolate Popcorn

12 oz. Package white chocolate morsels

3.3 oz. bag butter flavored microwave popcorn, popped

1/2 tsp. Ground cinnamon

1 cup salted mixed nuts

1 cup dried cranberries

Prepare the microwave popcorn, and place in a large bowl. Discard any unpopped kernels, and then add in the cranberries and nuts. In a microwave safe bowl, place the white chocolate morsels, heat on high for 1 1/2 minutes until the mixture is melted and smooth, stirring every 30 seconds. Pour this mixture over the popcorn till well coated. Spread in a single layer in a 15x10 inch jelly roll pan. Sprinkle on the cinnamon. Let stand at room temperature for 15 minutes until it hardens, then separate into pieces. Serve immediately or store in an airtight container. Makes 9 servings.

## Gingered Orange Almonds

1 tsp. Ground ginger

1 tbs. Orange juice

3 tsp. Grated orange peel

3 cups whole unblanched almonds

2/3 cup sugar

1 tsp. Ground cinnamon

1/2 tsp. Ground allspice

1 large egg white

In a bowl, mix the orange peel, sugar, all spice, cinnamon, and the ginger. In a separate bowl, combine the egg white with the orange juice. Stir in the almonds, coating them thoroughly. Sprinkle the sugar mixture over the almonds, tossing them well. Spread in a single layer on a baking sheet, baking at 300 degrees for 20-25 minutes. Transfer to wax paper to cool completely. Makes 3 1/2 cups.

## Holiday Spiced Pecans

2 cups pecans

1/2 tsp. Cayenne pepper

1 large egg white

2 tsp. Ground cinnamon

3/4 tsp. Ground ginger

1/4 tsp. Ground cloves

Salt to taste

Preheat the oven to 325 degrees. Line a rimmed baking sheet with parchment paper. In a bowl, whisk the egg white until foamy, add in the ginger, cinnamon, cloves, and cayenne. Stir in the nuts, and toss coating them well. Spread the nuts in a single layer on the baking sheet. Bake 15-20 minutes till the nuts are dry. Let cool completely, then season with salt. Store in an airtight container. Makes 8 servings.

## Noel Cranberry Chex Mix

1/2 cup dried cranberries

3 cups Corn Chex cereal

3 cups Rice Chex cereal

3 cups Wheat Chex cereal

1/4 cup frozen orange juice concentrate, thawed

1 cup sliced almonds

1/4 cup butter

1/4 cup brown sugar

Preheat the oven to 300 degrees. In a large mixing bowl, combine the cereals and the almonds. Using a 1 cup microwaveable measuring cup, place the butter, and cover. Microwave on high for 40 seconds until it is melted. Add in the brown sugar and the orange juice concentrate. Microwave uncovered for 30 seconds, and mix well. Pour this mixture over the cereal mixture, and combine till well coated. Spread in a single layer on an ungreased roasting pan. Bake uncovered for 25-30 minutes, stirring halfway. Add in the dried cranberries. Transfer to wax paper to cool completely, then store in airtight container. Makes 10 cups.

# Christmas recipes

## (1) White Christmas Rocky Road

Chewy rose flavor Turkish delight combines with marshmallows, nuts, and dried fruit to make the best Rocky Road recipe ever!

Serving Size: **25 pieces**

Preparation Time: **3hours 20mins**

Ingredient List:

- 17½ ounces white choc chips
- 3½ ounces whole macadamia nuts
- 2½ ounces unsalted pistachio nuts (shelled)
- ¾ cup dried cranberries
- 1½ cups mallows (cut into ⅓" discs)
- 7 ounces rose-flavored Turkish delight (quartered lengthwise)
- ½ cup shredded coconut

**Instructions:**

1. Double line an 8" square baking tin with aluminium foil.

2. Place the mallows, Turkish delight along with the shelled pistachios, cranberries, and shredded coconut in a large mixing bowl.

3. Melt the choc chips using a double boiler. Stir until silky smooth.

4. Pour the melted white chocolate over the marshmallow-coconut mixture in the bowl and gently but quickly fold in the melted white chocolate, ensuring that the mixture is evenly coated.

5. Pour the mixture into the baking tin and using your rubber utensil evenly spread the mixture.

6. Set aside at room temperature, for 2-3 hours until set.

7. When the rocky road has set, cut it into even sized squares, taking care not to crush the nuts and berries.

8. Gift package and present your gift.

## (2) Sparkling Sugar Plums

Although sugar plums have been more or less obsolete for more than 100 years, the word conjures up visions of traditional Christmas joy.

**Serving Size:** 40 sugar plums

Preparation Time: **1hour**

Ingredient List:

- 6 ounces slivered almonds
- 4 ounces dried plums (prunes)
- 2 ounces dried cherries (sweetened)
- 2 ounces Turkish apricots
- 2 ounces currants
- 2 ounces dried sweetened cranberries
- ¼ teaspoons each anise seeds, fennel seeds, caraway seeds, ground cardamom
- ¼ cup confectioner's sugar
- ⅛ teaspoons kosher salt
- ¼ cup organic honey
- 1 cup multi-colored sparkling sugar*

***Instructions:***

1. In a large skillet over moderate to high heat, toast the slivered almonds, stirring frequently, until golden and fragrant.

2. Take the skillet off the heat and cool to room temp.

3. Once the nuts are cool, place them along with the plums, dried cherries, Turkish apricots, currants, and cranberries in a food processor. Pulse, until granulated. The mixture needs to hold together.

4. Add the spices; anise seeds, together with the fennel, caraway, and ground cardamom to the dry skillet and over moderate to high heat allow the spices to toast lightly, for a couple of minutes, frequently stirring. Once fragrant, take off the heat.

5. In a mixing bowl, whisk the confectioners' sugar, spices, and salt together until full combined.

6. Add the fruit-nut mixture along with the honey to the bowl and using damp, clean hands, mix until incorporated.

7. Scatter the multi-colored sparkling sugar to a bowl. Using a heaped teaspoon, scoop the fruit mixture and gently roll it between the palms of your hand, to make a (1" diameter) ball shape.

8. Carefully, and evenly roll the balls in the sparkling sugar and transfer to a wire baking to dry.

*Use these products sparingly as they are not recommended for daily use and read the directions and warnings thoroughly before using.

# (3) Homemade Hazelnut and Chocolate Spread

A homemade of a childhood favorite is super delicious spread on toast or as a cake filling. A fantastic gourmet gift for a loved one.

***Serving Size:*** 1 (16 ounce) jar

Preparation Time: ***22mins***

Ingredient List:

- ½ cup hazelnuts (blanched)
- 3½ ounces dark 72% chocolate (roughly chopped)
- ⅓ cup + 2 tablespoons sweetened condensed milk
- 1½ tablespoons hazelnut oil
- ⅛ teaspoons sea salt
- 3½ tablespoons hot water

***Instructions:***

1. Preheat the main oven to 350 degrees F.

2. Arrange the hazelnuts on a baking sheet and place in the oven for between 5-8 minutes, until lightly golden and toasted.

3. Take the nuts out of the oven and allow to cool a little.

4. Transfer the warm nuts to a food processor and process to a smooth paste.

5. In a small-sized saucepan, over low heat, melt the chopped dark chocolate, along with the milk and oil.

6. Stir the mixture until silky smooth and add to the food processor with the hazelnut paste.

7. Add the sea salt and process, next add the water and process until the consistency is thick but easily spreadable.

8. When cool, transfer to a re-sealable jar, seal with a tight-fitting lid and label*.

How to pot spreads:

- All storage jars must be fastidiously clean, dry and sterilized. You can achieve this by washing the jars and lids in boiling soapy water and thoroughly rinsing.
- Place the open end of the jar facing upwards on a baking tray and heat in the oven at 275 degrees F, for 12-15 minutes until totally dry.
- When potting jam and preserves, immediately while hot, cover the filled jar with a wax disc, wax siding facing downwards; this prevents mold forming. Place a sterilized lid on the jar while the contents are still hot.
- Name and date the preserve and once opened store in a cool place.

# (4) Bacon and Caramelized Onion Jam

Salty bacon and sweet caramelized onions make a divine savory jam that will be devoured in no time.

Serving Size: **3 cups jam**

Preparation Time: **1hour 15mins**

Ingredient List:

- 1½ pounds bacon (chopped fine)
- 3 large white onion (chopped fine)
- 1 medium fresh leek (chopped fine)
- 2 garlic cloves (minced)
- ¼ teaspoons sea salt
- ½ cup good quality balsamic vinegar
- ½ cup light brown sugar
- ½ teaspoons oregano
- ¼ teaspoons ground nutmeg
- ½ teaspoons black pepper

*Instructions:*

1. Cook the chopped bacon for half an hour over medium heat in a deep, large skillet until crispy.

2. Use a slotted spoon to move the bacon from the skillet and set to one side on a paper towel-lined plate.

3. Drain away all but 2 tablespoons of bacon fat from the skillet.

4. Sauté the onion, leek, minced garlic and salt in the bacon fat.

5. Cook for 50 minutes until the onions have softened and caramelized.

6. Add the balsamic, brown sugar, oregano, nutmeg and black pepper along with the set-aside bacon.

7. Cook for a final 15 minutes.

8. Transfer the cooked jam to a food processor and blitz until mostly smooth and just a little chunky.

9. Allow to cool completely before spooning into re-sealable jars*.

* How to pot preserves:

- All storage jars must be fastidiously clean, dry and sterilized. You can achieve this by washing the jars and lids in boiling soapy water and thoroughly rinsing.
- Place the open end of the jar facing upwards on a baking tray and heat in the oven at 275 degrees F, for 12-15 minutes until totally dry.
- When potting jam and preserves, immediately while hot, cover the filled jar with a wax disc, wax siding facing downwards; this prevents mold forming. Place a sterilized lid on the jar while the contents are still hot.
- Name and date the preserve and once opened store in a cool place.

# (5) Vanilla Grapefruit Shortbread

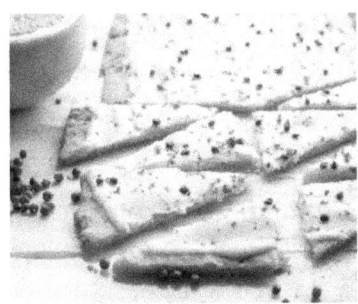

Grapefruit has a vibrant, refreshing and sometimes bitter flavor; sweet, creamy vanilla complements it perfectly.

**Serving Size:** 16 triangles shortbread

Preparation Time: **1hour**

Ingredient List:

- ½ cup + extra unsalted butter (chopped, softened)
- 1 tablespoon grapefruit zest (finely grated)
- 1 teaspoon vanilla essence
- ⅓ cup + 1 cup confectioner's sugar
- 1 cup all-purpose flour
- ½ teaspoons + extra sea salt
- 2 tablespoons freshly squeezed grapefruit juice

**Instructions:**

1. Lightly grease a 9" springform baking pan.

2. Add the butter, zest, vanilla and ⅓ confectioner's sugar into a food processor. Pulse until the ingredients come together.

3. Add the flour and sea salt and pulse until you have a just-combined dough.

4. Press the dough into the greased pan and use the bottom of a glass to smooth the surface.

5. Refrigerate for an hour.

6. Preheat main oven to 350 degrees F.

7. Remove the dough from the refrigerator and prick with a fork.

8. Place in the oven and bake for just over 15 minutes, until pale but golden at the edges.

9. When cooked, immediately remove the band from the springform pan and slice into 16 equal pieces (in the same way you would a pizza). Set aside to cool completely.

10. In a small bowl, whisk together the grapefruit juice, pinch sea salt and 1 cup confectioner's sugar until super smooth.

11. Spread an even layer of the grapefruit icing over the cooled shortbread, leaving a ½-1cm border un-iced.

12. Set aside to set for 15-20 minutes before retracing the slice marks and transferring to a re-sealable container.

## (6) Boozy Christmas Cupcakes

Dense, rich and indulgent these brandy infused Christmas cupcakes are an ideal yuletide gift.

Serving Size: **14**

Preparation Time: **1hour 20mins**

Ingredient List:

For the boozy fruit/nut mix:

- ⅔ cup strawberry jam
- ½ cup fruit and peel mix
- ¼ cup candied ginger
- 12 whole Medjool dates (pitted)
- ⅔ cup raisins
- ⅔ cup pecans
- ¼ teaspoons cardamom
- ⅛ teaspoons cloves
- ⅛ teaspoons nutmeg
- ½ teaspoons cinnamon
- 3 teaspoons rosewater
- 2 teaspoons vanilla essence
- 2 teaspoons molasses
- ⅓ cup pure maple syrup
- ⅓ cup brandy

*Batter:*

- ½ cup light brown sugar
- ¾ cup Spelt flour
- 1 stick butter (softened)
- 3 medium eggs

*Instructions:*

1. For the boozy fruit/nut mix: Add all ingredients to a bowl and mix until incorporated. Cover the bowl and place in a cool and dry place for 3-4 days.

2. For the boozy cupcakes: On day four, preheat the main oven to 300 degrees F.

3. Place the boozy fruit-spice mix in a food processor and pulse 2-3 times.

4. Next, add the brown sugar, along with the Spelt flour, butter, and eggs to the processor and pulse until incorporated.

5. Spoon the mixture into a lined cupcake tray and bake in the oven for 40-50 minutes.

6. Allow the cupcakes to cool.

# (7) Teacher's Treat

Your little ones will love giving Apple Pie in a Jar to their favorite teacher.

Serving Size: **_7 jars_**

Preparation Time: **_1hour 5mins_**

Ingredient List:

- Hot water
- 4½ cups white sugar
- 1 cup cornstarch
- 2 teaspoons ground cinnamon
- ¼ teaspoons ground nutmeg
- 1 teaspoon salt
- 10 cups water
- 3 tablespoons freshly squeezed lemon juice
- 7 quarts green apples (peeled, cored, sliced)

**_Instructions:_**

1. Place a rack in the bottom of a stock pot and fill with hot water.

2. Next, sterilize 7 (1 quart) canning jars, along with their lids, and rings; the jars need to stand upright. Bring the water to boil and boil for 10 minutes. Carefully, using tongs remove the jars and allow them to air dry. Retain the water for processing the apples.

3. In a large sized pan combine the white sugar along with the cornstarch, ground cinnamon, ground nutmeg, salt and 10 cups of water. Place the pan over a high heat and cook until the mixture begins to thicken and bubble, frequently stirring. Remove the pan from the heat and add the lemon juice, while stirring.

4. Tightly pack the slices of apples into each of the jars, make sure you compact them by pushing down with the handle of a wooden spoon.

5. Pour the syrup over the top of the apple slices, making sure that you completely cover them. Carefully taps each jar on the kitchen countertop; this allows the bubbles to rise. Screw the lids onto the jars.

6. Using a holder, carefully lower each jar into the stock pot, allowing a 2" space between each jar.

7. Add additional boiling water if needed, until the water covers the tops of the jar by 2". Bring the water to full boiling point, and cover. Cook for 30 minutes.

8. Remove the jars from the pot and place them on a heatproof surface.

9. Once the jars are cool, press the top of each lid using your index finger, to ensure that the seal is sufficiently tight.

10. Jars correctly sealed can be stored for up to 12 months.

# (8) Brandied Fruit

This recipe needs to be made well in advance, ideally at least 4 weeks before you intend to gift a jar. In fact, the longer you allow it to stand the stronger the flavor.

*Serving Size:* 8 (16 ounce) jars

*Preparation Time:* 15mins (4 weeks standing time)

Ingredient List:

- 2 cups fresh peaches (peeled, pitted, diced)
- 4 cups cherries (pitted, diced)
- 3 cups plums (pitted, diced)
- 5 cups granulated sugar
- 5 cups light brown sugar
- 4 cups good quality brandy

*Instructions:*

1. Combine the fruits with the sugars in a mixing bowl and toss well to coat. Cover the bowl and allow to macerate for 60 minutes, tossing at 15-minute intervals.

2. Equally, divide the fruits between 8 sterilized 1-pint jars.*

3. Pour in the brandy, making sure to submerge all of the fruit. Store in a cool place, covered, for at least 28 days.

4. Once sufficiently aged, keep the jars on the countertop. As the contents begin to diminish, top with additional fruit (ratio: 2 cups of fruit: to ½ cup white and brown sugar) and brandy to cover.

*How to pot preserves:

- All storage jars must be fastidiously clean, dry and sterilized. You can achieve this by washing the jars and lids in boiling soapy water and thoroughly rinsing.
- Place the open end of the jar facing upwards on a baking tray and heat in the oven at 275 degrees F, for 12-15 minutes until totally dry.
- When potting jam and preserves, immediately while hot, cover the filled jar with a wax disc, wax siding facing downwards; this prevents mold forming. Place a sterilized lid on the jar while the contents are still hot.
- Name, date and once opened, store in a cool place.

## (9) Snowball Truffles

Snowball truffles make the best Christmas candy treat ever!

Serving Size: **8-10**

Preparation Time: **15mins**

Ingredient List:

- ¼ cup sweetened condensed milk
- ⅛ teaspoons kosher salt
- 1 teaspoon vanilla essence
- 1 cup confectioner's sugar
- 1 cup shredded coconut (sweetened)
- 8 ounces semisweet baking chocolate (melted)

Coconut Topping:

- ¼ cup shredded coconut
- 2 drops pink food gel

***Instructions:***

1. In a bowl, combine the condensed milk along with the kosher salt, and vanilla essence. Add the confectioner's sugar and stir until combined. Add the sweetened shredded coconut and stir until incorporated.

2. Shape 1 tablespoon of mixture into a ball, rolling between clean palms.

3. Place the balls on a cookie sheet.

4. When the truffles are ready, place the cookie sheet in the fridge to chill for approximately 30 minutes; this will help them hold their shape.

5. In the meantime, prepare the topping. Place the coconut and food gel in a small bowl. Stir until an even color is achieved.

6. Carefully, and using a fork, dip the chilled coconut balls into the melted baking chocolate. Once the truffles are coated tap the fork against the bowl to remove any excess chocolate.

7. Place the truffles on a plate and transfer them to the refrigerator to set.

# (10) Cabernet Cranberry and Blueberry Sauce

You can never have enough cranberry sauce, and this gourmet gift is going to keep on giving for at least two weeks.

***Serving Size:*** 2 (10 ounce jars)

Preparation Time: ***30 minutes***

Ingredient List:

- 1 (8 ounce) bag fresh cranberries
- 6 ounces frozen blueberries (not thawed)
- 1 cup cabernet sauvignon
- 1 cup granulated sugar
- 1 tablespoon cinnamon,
- 1 teaspoon ground cloves

***Instructions:***

1. In a large kettle, combine all 6 ingredients and bring to rolling boil, intermittently stirring. Ensure that the kettle has sufficient room to allow the sauce to triple in volume. (The mixture will foam, and it can easily overflow)

2. Reduce to low heat and allow the sauce to simmer for between 20-30 minutes, or until it has slightly thickened and

reduced, and the majority of the berries have burst. Remember that the sauce will thicken as it begins to cool.

3. Transfer the sauce to sterilized, heatproof jars with lids.*

4. Allow the sauce to cool before refrigerating. When cooled to room temperature store in the fridge**.

5. Name, label, date, and gift!

**Refrigerated sauce will keep for up to 14 days.

*How to pot preserves:

- All storage jars must be fastidiously clean, dry and sterilized. You can achieve this by washing the jars and lids in boiling soapy water and thoroughly rinsing.
- Place the open end of the jar facing upwards on a baking tray and heat in the oven at 275 degrees F, for 12-15 minutes until totally dry.
- When potting jam and preserves, immediately while hot, cover the filled jar with a wax disc, wax siding facing downwards; this prevents mold forming. Place a sterilized lid on the jar while the contents are still hot.
- Name, date and once opened, store in a cool place.

# (11) Silver Star Ginger Cookies

You are sure to be the star of the show when you present this thoughtful gift.

Serving Size: **25-30**

Preparation Time: **1hour 10mins**

Ingredient List:

- ¾ stick salted butter (room temperature)
- 3½ ounces caster sugar
- 1 large egg
- 1 teaspoon ground ginger
- 7 ounces plain flour +more for sprinkling
- ½ teaspoons baking powder
- ½ teaspoons fine salt
- Edible silver dust*

*Instructions:*

1. Preheat the main oven to 350 degrees F. Line 1 or 2 baking trays with parchment paper.

2. In a large mixing bowl, cream the salted butter with the caster sugar. Beat in the egg, followed by the ground ginger, plain flour, baking powder, and fine salt and mix until soft dough forms.

3. Mold the dough into 2 discs, wrapping each disc in plastic wrap and place in the refrigerator for 25-30 minutes.

4. Lay 1 dough disk on a clean work surface lightly dusted with flour. Sprinkle the disc with a little extra flour and roll out to a thickness of no more than ¼".

5. Using a star shape cutter, cut the dough into star shapes. Remember to dip the cutter in flour each time you cut a new shape.

6. Lay the cookies, not touching each other and with a little space between each one on the parchment lined baking tray(s).

7. Keep any leftover scraps and re-roll, until all of the dough has been used.

8. Bake in the preheated for between 15-20 minutes, depending on their thickness, until they are soft in the center, and lightly golden around the edges.

9. Remove the baking tray(s) from the oven, and using a flexible but flat utensil transfer the cookies to wire baking rack to cool; they will harden as they cool. Dip a small, clean brush in the edible silver dust and gild each star.

*Use these products sparingly as they are not recommended for daily use and read the directions and warnings thoroughly before using.

# (12) Candy Cane Chocolate Fudge

This chocolate fudge makes a wonderful edible gift, which is suitable for all ages.

Serving Size: **64**

Preparation Time: **4hours 20mins**

Ingredient List:

- 4 cup bittersweet chocolate chips
- 2 cans sweetened condensed milk
- 1 tablespoon unsalted butter (cold)
- 2 teaspoons pure vanilla extract
- ¼ teaspoons kosher salt
- ¾ cup candy canes (crushed)

***Instructions:***

1. Line 2 (8") square baking pans with aluminium foil, allow an overhang on 2 sides of the pan.

2. Using a small sized pan, combine the bittersweet chocolate chips with the milk. Cook over low heat, frequently stirring, until the chocolate is silky smooth and the chocolate completely melted.

3. Add the cold butter along with the vanilla extract and kosher salt to the pan and stir well until the butter is melted and incorporated.

4. Evenly spread the mixture into the prepared baking pans and sprinkle generously with crushed candy canes.

5. Transfer to the refrigerator until firm, for 3-4 hours.

6. Using the overhanging foil, transfer the candy cane fudge to a chopping board and cut into even 1" squares.

## (13) Silver and Gold Dust Date Truffles

Nothing says Merry Christmas more than a pretty box of decadent silver and gold truffles.

**Serving Size:** 20 truffles

Preparation Time: **3hours 8mins**

Ingredient List:

- 3½ ounces Medjool dates
- 7 ounces almonds
- 1½ tablespoons raw cacao powder
- ½ teaspoons vanilla powder
- 2-3 tablespoons virgin coconut oil

- Zest of 1 large organic orange
- Edible silver and gold decorating dust*

**Instructions:**

1. First, soften the dates but putting them in a mixing bowl and soaking them in boiling water for 5 minutes. Drain and set to one side.

2. Put the almonds in food blender or processor and pulse until you achieve an almond flour consistency.

3. Next, add the drained dates along with the cacao powder, vanilla powder, coconut oil and orange zest. Continue blending until you the dough is a greasy consistency.

4. Using your hands shape the mixture into small even shaped truffle shape balls. Arrange the truffles on a plate and cover with parchment paper. Transfer the truffles to the fridge for 2-3 hours.

5. When chilled roll the truffles alternately in silver and gold dust.

*Use these products sparingly as they are not recommended for daily use and read the directions and warnings thoroughly before using.

# (14) Cherry Espresso Biscotti

Enjoy these delicious espresso and cherry biscotti with after-dinner coffee. The ideal gift to take to a dinner party or get together.

**Serving Size:** 40 biscotti

Preparation Time: **1hour**

Ingredient List:

- 4 tablespoons powdered espresso
- 1 tablespoon vanilla essence
- 2½ cups all-purpose flour
- 1 cup granulated sugar
- 2 teaspoons baking powder
- ¼ teaspoons sea salt
- 3 eggs (beaten lightly)
- ¾ cup toasted walnuts (chopped)
- ¾ cup cherries (dried)

**Instructions:**

1. Preheat main oven to 350 degrees F. Line 2 rimmed baking sheets with parchment.

2. In a bowl combine the powdered espresso and vanilla essence.

3. In a separate bowl, add the flour, granulated sugar, baking powder and sea salt. Whisk to combine. Add the egg and espresso mixture to the dry ingredients and whisk until combined.

4. Fold through the chopped walnuts and dried cherries.

5. Divide the dough evenly between the 2 baking sheets.

6. Roll each half of 2ough into a 2.5" wide x 0.75" high, log.

7. Bake in the oven for just over 20 minutes. Set aside to cool for 18-22 minutes, on a wire rack before slicing each log into 0.25" diagonal slices, using a bread knife.

8. Arrange the sliced biscotti on the same 2 baking sheets and return to the oven for a final 15 minutes, flipping the biscuits over halfway through baking.

9. Allow to cool completely before transferring to an airtight container.

## (15) Pumpkin Spice Whipped Honey Butter

This spiced whipped butter is bursting with festive flavor and is delightful when generously spread over pastries and cookies.

***Serving Size:*** 1½ cups whipped butter

Preparation Time: ***10mins***

Ingredient List:

- 1 cup salted butter (room temperature)
- ¾ teaspoons ground cinnamon
- 6 tablespoons pumpkin puree
- 4 tablespoons organic honey
- 1 teaspoon vanilla essence

***Instructions:***

1. Add the butter to the bowl of a stand mixer. Beat until smooth.

2. Add the cinnamon and pumpkin puree. Beat until incorporated.

3. Add the honey and vanilla essence and beat until the butter, is fluffy, thick and whippy.

4. Transfer to a re-sealable container and refrigerate.

## (16) Chocolate Coated Cherries

A gorgeous gourmet gift for your favorite person.

***Serving Size:*** Approx. 30 cherries

Preparation Time: ***40mins***

Ingredient List:

- 1 (10 ounce) jar maraschino cherries with stems (reserve juice)
- 3-4 cups confectioner's sugar (divided)
- ½ stick butter (softened)
- ½ teaspoons almond essence
- 12 ounces dark melting chocolate

***Instructions:***

1. Position a colander over a mixing bowl, drain the cherries, reserving their juice.

2. Transfer the drained cherries to a sheet of kitchen paper towel; this will absorb any excess liquid.

3. In a medium-sized mixing bowl, combine 1 cup confectioner's sugar along with the softened butter, ¼ cup cherry juice, and almond essence. Beat well using an electric mixer until incorporated.

4. Add an additional 2 cups of powdered sugar and beat well until the mixture is a soft dough, a little sticky, and the consistency of a thick frosting. You can add more sugar in ¼ cups until the dough is the correct consistency. Transfer the dough to the refrigerator for 25 minutes.

5. Roll the dough into 1" balls and using the palms of clean hands, gently flatten the balls. Dust your palms with powdered sugar if needed.

6. Put a cherry in the middle of each dough round, then fold the dough up over the cherry to cover, leaving only the stem uncovered.

7. Place the cherries in the fridge for 25 minutes.

8. Using a double boiler, melt the chocolate.

9. Hold each cherry by its stem and dip it into the melted chocolate, allowing any excess to drip off. Repeat the process until all cherries are dipped.

10. Transfer the chocolate coated cherries to a baking tray, covered with waxed paper. Allow the chocolate to set completely.

11. Store the chocolate coated cherries in an airtight, re-sealable container at room temperature. The center of the cherries will become soft and liquefy in 3-5 days.

## (17) Pixie Dusted White Chocolate Almonds

Christmas almonds make the perfect homemade edible gift.

Serving Size: *1*

Preparation Time: *25mins*

Ingredient List:

- 1 ounce white choc chips
- 3½ ounces raw almonds
- Edible multicolored glitter*
- Food dye** (optional)

**Instructions:**

1. Use a double boiler to melt the white choc chips
2. Line a baking sheet or tray with parchment paper.
3. Using a small clean brush to coat half of each almond with the melted white chocolate.
4. Transfer the almonds to the lined baking sheet.
5. Set the chocolate coated almonds to one side for a couple of minutes, to dry.
6. Sprinkle with edible glitter.
7. Set the glitter-dusted almonds to one side for 15-20 minutes, or until completely dry.

*Use these products sparingly as they are not recommended for daily use and read the directions and warnings thoroughly before using.

**You can add 1 or 2 drops of food dye to the white chocolate if you prefer colored almonds.

## (18) Chocolate Dipped Licorice

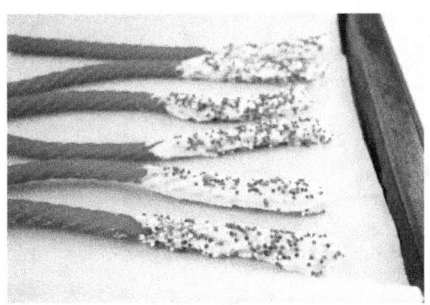

Licorice dipped in chocolate is a popular Icelandic candy, and it makes a truly tasty edible gift.

Serving Size: *1 bag*

Preparation Time: **1hour**

Ingredient List:

- 2 cups semi-sweet chocolate chips
- 1 (24 ounce) bag soft black licorice twists
- Red, Green and white sprinkles

**Instructions:**

1. In a microwave-safe bowl, carefully melt the chocolate chips in the microwave, making sure then don't burn.

2. Cut the licorice twists into two.

3. Dip the cut ends into the melted chocolate, coating to around 1" up each twist.

4. Transfer each chocolate covered twist onto a waxed paper lined, rimmed cookie tray, arranging the twists in single rows.

5. Scatter the chocolate end of each twist with a mix of red, green and white sprinkles

6. Put the rimmed cookie sheet in the freezer for 20-30 minutes, or until the chocolate hardens.

7. Remove the twists from the freezer and place in a cellophane bag.

# (19) Peppermint Cracker Toffee

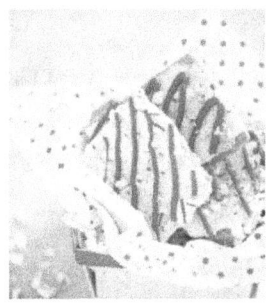

Your friends and family will go crackers for this tempting toffee.

Serving Size: **40**

Preparation Time: **20mins**

Ingredient List:

- 40 saltine crackers
- 1 cup unsalted butter
- 1 cup granulated sugar
- 1 (11 ounce) package white choc chips
- 6 candy canes (crushed)

*Instructions:*

1. Line a 15x10x1" baking tray with parchment paper. Preheat the main oven to 375 degrees F.

2. Arrange the saltines in a single layer on the baking tray.

3. In a small-sized saucepan over moderate to high heat, melt the unsalted butter.

4. Add the granulated sugar and bring to boil, continually stirring. As soon as the mixture comes to boil, take the saucepan off the heat.

5. Pour the mixture over the saltines and place in the oven for 10-12 minutes, or until the crackers are caramelized and golden.

6. Scatter with white choc chips and allow to rest for 5-7 minutes.

7. Evenly spread the mixture over the crackers and sprinkle with the crushed candy canes.

8. Allow to set and store in a re-sealable container for up to 4-5 days.

## (20) Chocolate Peppermint Spoons

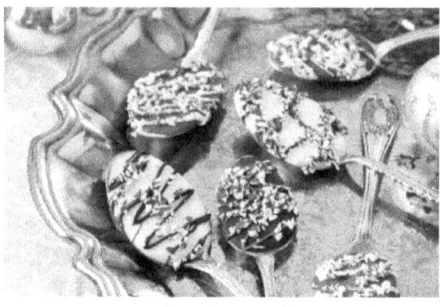

These chocolate coated spoons are the ideal gift for anyone who is a hot chocolate or coffee lover. Simply dip the spoon into a hot drink and get an extra chocolate boost.

Serving Size: **12 spoons**

Preparation Time: **1 hour**

Ingredient List:

- ½ cup dark chocolate chips
- ¼ cup peppermint crunch baking chips
- Special equipment:
- 12 wooden teaspoons

*Instructions:*

1. Line a baking tray or sheet with parchment paper and put to one side.

2. Using a double boiler, gently melt the dark chocolate.

3. Carefully, dip each spoon into the melted chocolate and lay on the parchment paper, making sure that they don't touch one another.

4. Sprinkle with peppermint crunch baking chips.

5. Allow the spoons to chill and set.

6. Wrap in cellophane.

## (21) Passionfruit Caramels

Soft, chewy and fruity, these caramels are to die for.

Serving Size: **60-70**

Preparation Time: **14hours 50mins**

Ingredient List:

- 1½ cups granulated sugar
- ½ cup heavy cream
- ½ cup pureed passionfruit
- 4 tablespoons unsalted butter

- 2 tablespoons corn syrup
- ½ teaspoons sea salt
- ½ teaspoons vanilla bean extract or paste

***Instructions:***

1. Line an 8" square baking pan with parchment paper.

2. In a large-sized pot, fitted with a candy thermometer, combine the granulated sugar along with the heavy cream, pureed passionfruit, unsalted butter, corn syrup, and sea salt. Over high heat, while stirring, bring to boil. Continue stirring until the sugar dissolves; using a damp pastry brush, brush any sugar crystals off the side of the pot.

3. Reduce to moderate to high heat and continue boiling, while not stirring, until the mixture registers 252 degrees F this will take around 15-20 minutes.

4. Remove the pot from the heat and add the vanilla extract, stir to combine.

5. Immediately, pour the mixture into the prepared baking pan and allow to rest, uncovered, at room temperature for a minimum of 12-14 hours, or until firmly set.

6. Using the parchment paper as a handle carefully lift the caramel out of the baking pan and using a sharp kitchen knife cut the caramel into 1¼" strips, and crosswise into ¾" pieces.

7. Wrap each caramel with cellophane wrappers.

8. These caramels can be stored in an airtight container for up to 28 days.

# (22) Cinnamon Spiced Candied Pecans

These moreish nuts are impossible to stop eating. You'll undoubtedly be inundated with requests for a refill.

***Serving Size:*** 11 ounces candied nuts

Preparation Time: ***45mins***

Ingredient List:

- 1 egg white
- 1 tablespoon cold water
- 5⅓ ounces caster sugar
- 1 teaspoon ground cinnamon
- 1 teaspoon sea salt
- ¼ teaspoons vanilla essence
- 10½ ounces whole pecans

***Instructions:***

1. Preheat main oven to 340 degrees F. Line a baking sheet with parchment.

2. Whisk together the egg white and cold water until it forms a semi-stiff froth.

3. Add the caster sugar, ground cinnamon, sea salt and vanilla essence to the egg, stir gently.

4. Add the pecans to a large bowl and pour the egg/sugar mixture over the top. Toss until the pecans are well coated.

5. Arrange the coated pecans on the baking sheet in a single layer.

6. Bake in the oven for half an hour, removing halfway through baking to toss the nuts.

7. Allow to cool before transferring to re-sealable jars*.

*Candied nuts in sealed jars will keep for up to 14 days at room temperature.

## (23) Nonna's Homemade Limoncello

There's no better way to finish a meal than with a small glass of homemade limoncello, just like nonna makes!

**Serving Size:** 4 (6 ounce) bottles limoncello

Preparation Time: **4 days 30mins**

Ingredient List:

- 2 pounds fresh lemons (washed)
- 1 (25 ounce) bottle grain alcohol or vodka

- 6 cups filtered water
- 2½ cups granulated sugar

***Instructions:***

1. Peel the washed lemons and add into 2 large mason jars.

2. Pour the grain alcohol equally into both jars. Seal and shake.

3. Store the Kars in a cool, dry place returning occasionally to shake.

4. Strain the alcohol into an extra large pitcher, discarding the zest.

5. In a saucepan, add the water and sugar. Heat until the sugar dissolved. Stir well aside to completely cool.

6. Pour the cooled sugar syrup into the alcohol in the pitcher. Stir to combine and pour into pretty 6 ounces re-sealable bottles.

7. Store in the freezer until ready to gift.

## (24) Clementine Christmas Curd

This velvety smooth curd makes the ideal pressie for family and friends.

***Serving Size:*** 3 (13 ounce) jars

Preparation Time: ***40mins***

Ingredient List:
- Zest of 5 clementines (finely grated)
- Juice of 5 clementines
- 4 large eggs
- 12 ounces caster sugar (cut into cubes)
- 8 ounces salted butter (chilled, cubed)

**Instructions:**

1. Add the clementine zest and juice to a large heatproof bowl.

2. In a mixing bowl beat the eggs, add the fruit zest and juice along with the sugar and whisk to combine.

3. Set the mixing bowl over a saucepan of gently simmering water; the base of the mixing bowl must not touch the water in the pan.

4. Add the cubes of butter and cook over low heat, continually stirring until the curd begins to thicken and coats the back of a tablespoon; approximately 18-10 minutes.

5. Pour the curd immediately into a jar* and allow to cool**.

*How to pot preserves:

- All storage jars must be fastidiously clean, dry and sterilized. You can achieve this by washing the jars and lids in boiling soapy water and thoroughly rinsing.
- Place the open end of the jar facing upwards on a baking tray and heat in the oven at 275 degrees F, for 12-15 minutes until totally dry.
- When potting jam and preserves, immediately while hot, cover the filled jar with a wax disc, wax siding facing downwards; this prevents mold forming. Place a sterilized lid on the jar while the contents are still hot.

- Name and date the preserve and once opened store in a cool place.

**Clementine curd will keep for 28 days in a cool, dry place. Once opened, store in the refrigerator for up to 14 days.

## (25) Mulled Wine Kit

A do-it-yourself edible gift. Now your friends can join in the fun with this mulled wine kit.

*Serving Size:* 1 (5.4 ounce) jar / mulling for 6 bottles wine

Preparation Time: *5mins*

Ingredient List:

Spice Mix:

- 6 (3") cinnamon sticks (broken into small pieces)
- 6 whole star anise (broken into small pieces)
- 2 tablespoons whole allspice berries
- 2 tablespoons whole cloves
- 1 tablespoon green cardamom pods
- 1 teaspoon black peppercorns

*Assembly:*

- 1 medium orange
- 1 bottle red wine
- 6 (4x4") squares cheesecloth
- 6 (6") lengths string
- Printed or written mulling directions (see below)

**Instructions:**

1. In a bowl, add allspice mix ingredients and stir to combine. Transfer the mixture to a jar.

2. Present the gift, in a large gift bag, together with the orange, and wine.

3. Using the twine tie the cheesecloth into sachets and secure with string.

4. Add the mulling instructions (below) to your gift bag.

Mulling instructions (for 1 bottle):

Ingredient List:

- 1 tablespoon mulling spice mix (from the gift)
- 1 square of cheesecloth and twine
- 2 tablespoons organic honey
- Zest and fresh juice 1 medium orange
- 1 bottle of red wine.

**Instructions:**

1. Scoop 1 tablespoon of mulling mix into the middle of the cheesecloth square, gather each corner and secure with string.

2. In a large sized pan, combine the cheesecloth bag with the honey, orange zest, orange juice, and 1 bottle of red wine.

3. Heat the mulled wine mixture until beginning to steam, without boiling, stirring well to dissolve the sugar.

# (26) Coconut Lime Snowballs

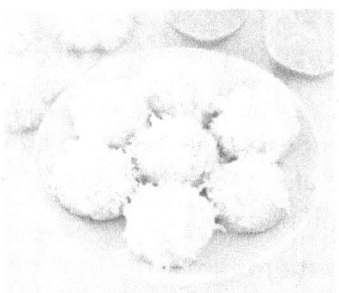

Delightful little balls of 'snow' tropically flavored with coconut and lime make a lovely festive gift.

***Serving Size:*** 48 snowballs

Preparation Time: ***2hours 40mins***

Ingredient List:

- 12 ounces nice quality white chocolate (roughly chopped)
- ¼ cup coconut oil (preferable virgin)
- 13½ ounces coconut milk (unsweetened)
- 1 tablespoon lime zest (finely grated)
- 12 teaspoons vanilla essence
- ¾ teaspoons sea salt
- tablespoons freshly squeezed lime juice
- 1½ cups shredded coconut (unsweetened)

***Instructions:***

1. Preheat main oven to 250 degrees F.
2. In a glass dish (9x13"), add the white chocolate and coconut oil.

3. Place in the oven and cook for 45-60 minutes, stirring every quarter of an hour. The mixture is ready when it is the same color as milky coffee. Set aside to cool a little.

4. In the meantime, pour the coconut milk into a saucepan and simmer over a low-medium heat for approximately 10 minutes, swirling the pan occasionally. Allow to cool al little.

5. Pour the slightly cooled milk over the chocolate mixture. Add the fresh lime juice, along with the vanilla essence and sea salt. Whisk well until combined and smooth.

6. Cover and refrigerate for an hour.

7. Combine the lime zest and shredded coconut in a bowl.

8. Remove the chocolate mix from the refrigerator and use a teaspoon to scoop a little of the mixture at a time. Using your hands, roll into a smooth bowl and cover in the lime/coconut mixture.

9. Arrange the finished snowballs on a baking sheet covered with parchment and refrigerate until set and store in a re-sealable Tupperware.

## (27) Mini Brie and Jam Pie

Not everyone has a sweet tooth, and this savory edible gift provides a welcome change.

Serving Size: **4**

Preparation Time:

Ingredient List:

- 2 cups all-purpose flour
- 1¾ stick unsalted butter (chilled, cubed)
- 1 tablespoon light brown sugar
- ½ teaspoons sea salt
- ½ cup ice-cold water
- 4 whole mini brie wheels (chilled)
- 12 tablespoons raspberry jam

**Instructions:**

1. Add the first 4 ingredients into a food processor and pulse until the butter is pea-sized.

2. Gradually, add ½ cup of ice-cold water (in ⅛ cup increments) and pulse until you have a dough.

3. Transfer the dough to a lightly floured work surface and evenly divide into 4 portions. Wrap the portions in plastic wrap and plate in the refrigerator.

4. In the meantime, remove the top and bottom skin (rind) of each mini brie.

5. On a lightly floured, clean work surface, roll out 1 portion of the dough to no more than ¼" thick.

6. Add 3 tablespoons of raspberry jam in the center of each portion of dough and then lay a mini brie on the top.

7. Fold the dough over to encase, remove excess dough as necessary and pinch the opening together, tightly.

8. Flip it over with the seam side facing down, wrap in plastic, and transfer to the refrigerator. Repeat the process with the remaining brie. Keep the brie and jam pies chilled.

9. To bake, preheat the main oven to 400 degrees F.

10. Using, a pastry brush, brush the whole surface, including the base, of the pies with egg wash and bake in the oven for 20-25 minutes, or until golden and browned.

11. If the base of the pie doesn't look sufficiently brown, place the pan directly on the base of the oven for final 5 minutes of baking.

12. Allow the pie to cool before wrapping in parchment along with a gift note.

## (28) Espresso Sugar Cubes

Get crafty with these fun caffeine-spiked sugar cubes.

***Serving Size:*** 1 bag (180 cubes)

Preparation Time: ***8hours 55mins***

Ingredient List:

- 1 tablespoon good quality powdered espresso
- 1½ teaspoons meringue powder
- 1½ teaspoons water (hot)
- 1½ cups white sugar
- Special equipment:

- 4x6" cellophane bag
- Jute bag

**Instructions:**

1. Preheat the main oven to 250 degrees F.

2. In a large mixing bowl, combine the powdered espresso along with the meringue powder and water. Whisk until lump free. Set to one side to cool.

3. Add the white sugar, whisk well until the mixture has damp sand-like consistency. Spoon half of the mixture into 2 mini silicon ice cube trays (each with 90 compartments) *.

4. Using a rubber kitchen utensil spread the mixture, firmly pressing it into the ice cube tray slots. Scrape away any excess sugar mixture, returning them to the mixing bowl. Repeat the process until all of the mixture is used.

5. Transfer the trays to a baking tray and bake in the oven for 40 minutes (food grade silicon is safe up to 500 degrees F. Check before purchase).

6. Allow the cubes to rest until hard, overnight, before turning out of the trays.

7. Next prepare the gift packaging. Take a black permanent marker pen and using letter stencils, write your gift message on a jute (5x7") bag.

8. Transfer the cubes to 4x6" cellophane bag, tie with a twist, and place inside the jute bag. Pull the string.

*These trays are inexpensive and can be easily found online.

# (29) Mince Pie Cookies

All the flavor of a fruity and buttery mince pie in a sweet little cookie. It doesn't get much more festive than this!

Serving Size: **84 cookies**

Preparation Time: **20mins**

Ingredient List:

- 7 ounces salted butter
- 11 ounces caster sugar
- 3 medium eggs
- ½ teaspoons vanilla essence
- 14 ounces plain flour
- 1 teaspoon sea salt
- 1 teaspoon bicarb of soda
- 4½ ounces whole walnuts (chopped)
- 15 ounces mince pie filling* (drained)

***Instructions:***

1. Preheat main oven to 355 degrees F. Grease multiple cookie sheets.

2. Cream together the salted butter, caster sugar and eggs. Add the vanilla essence and stir.

3. Sift together the plain flour, sea salt and bicarb of soda. Add the flour mixture into the butter mixture in batches and beat well after every addition, until just combined.

4. Fold through the walnuts and mince pie filling.

5. Use a teaspoon to drop equal sized amounts of cookie dough onto the prepared sheets.

6. Bake in the oven for just over 8 minutes.

7. Allow to cool completely before transferring to a re-sealable container.

*Also known as mincemeat.

## (30) Fruity Jellies

Bursting with berry and sharp apple flavor these sugar-dusted jellies make the ideal edible gift.

Serving Size: **36 jellies**

Preparation Time: **3hours**

Ingredient List:

- Sunflower oil (to grease)

- 1 pound frozen mixed summer berries
- 1 Granny Smith apple (peeled, cored, chopped)
- ¼ pint water
- 2 tablespoons freshly squeezed lemon juice
- 1 pound white sugar + extra for dusting
- 4 ounces pectin (liquid form)

***Instructions:***

1. Line a shallow 7" baking tin with parchment paper and lightly oil.

2. In a medium-sized saucepan, fitted with a candy thermometer, bring the mixed berries, chopped apple and ¼ pint of water to boil. Allow the water to bubble for approximately 10 minutes, or until the fruit is tender.

3. Remove the pan from the heat and with a stick blender, puree the fruit. Sieve the fruit using a fine mesh sieve and discard any pips.

4. Return the fruit puree to the saucepan along with the lemon juice and sugar.

5. Heat slowly, until the sugar dissolves. Increase the heat and boil, while frequently stirring for 20 minutes, until the mixture reaches 210 degrees F on the thermometer.

6. Remove the pan from the heat and add the pectin, stirring to combine.

7. Return the pan to the heat for 8-10 minutes, or until the mixture reads a temperature of 220 degrees F.

8. Carefully pour the jelly mixture into the prepared baking tin.

9. Scatter a little granulated sugar on top and put to one side to set, for 2-3 hours.

10. When set, turn the jelly out on a piece of parchment paper and using an oiled kitchen knife, cut the jelly into 36 neat, evenly sized squares.

11. Toss the squares with a little more granulated sugar, until evenly coated and arrange on a wire baking rack, overnight before transferring to a re-sealable airtight container*.

*The jellies can be stored in an airtight container for up to 14 days.

# (31) Mexican Spiced Hot Cocoa Jar Mix

This homemade instant hot cocoa mix layered in a pretty jar is the perfect winter gift for friends and family.

***Serving Size:*** 1 16-ounce jar of mix

Preparation Time: **45mins**

Ingredient List:

- ½ cup cocoa powder (unsweetened)
- ½ cup white sugar
- ½ teaspoons cayenne pepper
- 8 ounces Mexican chocolate (roughly chopped)
- 12 green cardamom pods
- 3 sticks cinnamon
- 1 vanilla bean (sliced lengthwise)
- 1 cup mini mallows

***Instructions:***

1. In a 16-ounce glass re-sealable jar neatly layer the first 7 ingredients in the order listed.

2. Cut a circle of parchment paper the same diameter as the jar and rest on top of the vanilla beans. Arrange the mallows on top

of the parchment to separate them from the remaining ingredients.

3. Seal the jar and decorate as desired!

# (32) Glitter Pops

These sparkly glitter lollipop favors are the perfect festive gifts for little ones, wrapped in individual clear cellophane bags and tied with a pretty bow.

Serving Size: **20-25**

Preparation Time:

Ingredient List:

- Edible glitters (red/green/gold) *
- 2 cups white sugar
- ⅔ cup light corn syrup
- ¼ cup water
- Iced water

**Special equipment:**

- Candy thermometer
- Lollipop sticks

*Instructions:*

1. First, prepare your kitchen work surface by laying strips of parchment paper directly onto the countertops.

2. Carefully, sprinkle the glitter in 3" circles approximately 3" apart in 2 rows; the lollipop sticks need to face in opposite directions and lay flat.

3. Add the sugar, along with the corn syrup and water in a saucepan with a spout, fitted with a candy thermometer and bring to boil, while constantly stirring, until the sugar is completely dissolved.

4. Once the syrup is boiling, take a dampened pastry brush and brush down the sides of the saucepan.

5. Do not stir, and boil until the syrup registers 300-310 degrees F, this will take between 6-8 minutes.

6. Remove the pan from the heat and set the pan in a large heatproof bowl, partly filled with iced water for no more than 15 seconds. This will remove the air bubbles without allowing the mixture to cool down too much which is important because it needs to be pourable.

7. Pour the mixture very carefully and slowly into the center of each glitter circle, until a round shape is formed. Gently press a lolly stick into the mixture.

8. Allow the lollipops to completely cool before gift wrapping.

*Use these products sparingly as they are not recommended for daily use and read the directions and warnings thoroughly before using.

# (33) Merry Muffin Mix in a Jar

Share the love of baking with this muffin mix present.

Serving Size: **12**

Preparation Time: **25mins**

Ingredient List:

For the jar:

- 1¾ cups plain flour
- 1 teaspoon bicarb of soda
- ¼ teaspoons kosher salt
- 1¼ cups light brown sugar
- ⅔ cup cocoa powder
- 1 cup milk choc chips
- 1 quart sized mason jar

***Instructions:***

1. Layer the ingredients, in the order listed, neatly inside the mason jar.

2. Add the lid to the jar, rim, and add a Christmas themed fabric square.

3. Attach a gift tag, listing the ingredients, and giving directions (see below) *.

*Instructions for the gift tag:

Ingredients needed:

- 2 large eggs
- 3/4 cup milk
- 2 teaspoons vanilla
- ½ cup vegetable oil

**Instructions:**

1. In a bowl, mix the eggs along with the milk, vanilla, and vegetable oil, stir until incorporated.

2. Add the dry ingredients, and stir until totally combined.

3. Line a 12 cup muffin tin, and line.

4. Fill the muffin cups to 75% full and bake in the oven at 350 degrees F for 15-20 minutes.

# (34) Glittery Strawberry Jam with Prosecco

Your friends and family will love topping their toast with a little seasonal sparkle.

Serving Size: **4 jars**

Preparation Time: **45mins**

Ingredient List:

- 1¾ pound fresh strawberries (hulled, mashed)
- 1 quart jam sugar
- 2 tablespoons salted butter
- 6¾ ounces Prosecco
- 1 (0.6 ounces) pot of edible gold glitter*

***Instructions:***

1. Place the strawberries in a heavy bottomed (4-5 quart) saucepan.

2. Add the jam sugar to the pan and heat gently, while continually stirring, until the sugar has dissolved. Do not allow to boil.

3. Add a dab of salted butter and stir to combine.

4. Next, pour in the Prosecco.

5. Turn the heat up and continue to stir until the jam bubbles and comes to a rolling boil. The mixture should rise in the saucepan, and it should not be possible to stir it down. Boil for 4 minutes.

6. Remove the pan from the heat and stir in the gold glitter until evenly distributed.

7. Working very speedily ladle the jam into jars**.

8. Tie a piece of Christmas ribbon around the top and pop on a gift tag.

*Use these products sparingly as they are not recommended for daily use and read the directions and warnings thoroughly before using.

**How to pot preserves:

- All storage jars must be fastidiously clean, dry and sterilized. You can achieve this by washing the jars and lids in boiling soapy water and thoroughly rinsed.
- Place the open end of the jar facing upwards on a baking tray and heat in the oven at 275 degrees F, for 12-15 minutes until totally dry.
- When potting jam and preserves, immediately while hot, cover the filled jar with a wax disc, wax siding facing downwards; this prevents mold forming. Place a sterilized lid on the jar while the contents are still hot.
- Name and date the preserve and once opened store in a cool place.

# (35) Marinated Feta Cheese

Salty feta cheese marinated in oregano, red onion, and red peppercorns will bring plenty of flavor to any salad or main dish.

Serving Size: **2 cups**

**Preparation Time:** 5mins (1-2 days marinating time)

Ingredient List:

- 1 pound good quality Greek feta cheese (drained, pat dry, cubed)
- ½ medium red onion (finely sliced)
- 1 tablespoon dried oregano
- 1 teaspoon whole red peppercorns
- Greek extra virgin olive oil

**Instructions:**

1. Arrange the feta cheese in a resealable glass jar, layering with the onion, oregano, and red peppercorns.

2. Pour over enough olive oil to completely cover the cheese. Seal the jar and refrigerate for at least 2 days before gifting to allow the flavors to intensify*.

*Marinated feta will keep for 5 days after marinating.

# (36) Golden Chilli Vodka

A perfect party gift or present for any occasion and time of the year.

Serving Size: **1 bottle**

Preparation Time: **2mins**

Ingredient List:

- 1 bottle good quality vodka
- 1 extra large red chili
- Large pinch gold leaf edible flakes*

*Instructions:*

1. Transfer the vodka to the bottle you wish to present it in.

2. Drop the chili pepper into the vodka and add the edible gold leaf flakes.

3. Shake the bottle to distribute the glitter.

4. Pop on a gift tag and present your gift.

*Use these products sparingly as they are not recommended for daily use and read the directions and warnings thoroughly before using.

# (37) Homemade Vanilla Extract

Do you know somebody who loves baking? Then spoil and impress them at the same time with a gift of homemade vanilla extract. Just be sure to prepare your extract with plenty of time to spare, as it takes around 2 months to 'brew.'

***Serving Size:*** 4 (4 ounce) bottles extract

***Preparation Time:*** 5mins (2 months brewing time)

Ingredient List:

- 6 vanilla beans
- 2 cups (80 proof) vodka
- Equipment:
- 4 (4 ounce) re-sealable glass bottles (washed with boiling water)

***Instructions:***

1. Slice each vanilla bean in half lengthways.

2. Place 3 halves of bean into each glass bottle. Use a funnel, or measuring jug with a lip, to pour ½ a cup of vodka into each bottle.

3. Seal and set aside in a cool, dark place for at least 2 months to 'brew' returning occasionally to shake the bottles.

# (38) Hibiscus Home Infused Vodka

The perfect gift for the foodie in your life, this herby salt is packed with flavor and will enhance and roast meat or potato dish.

**Serving Size:** 4 (25 ounce) bottles

Preparation Time: **6hours 5mins**

Ingredient List:

- 4 (25 ounce) bottles good quality vodka
- 8 organic hibiscus tea bags

**Instructions:**

1. Pour the vodka from the 4 bottles into an extra large pitcher.
2. Place the tea bags in the vodka and steep for 4-6 hours.
3. Remove the bags and strain the vodka back into the 4 bottles.
4. Seal and store in a dark, dry place until you are ready to gift.

# (39) Homemade Herby Salt

The perfect gift for the foodie in your life, this herby salt is packed with flavor and will enhance and roast meat or potato dish.

**Serving Size:** approx. 3 cups salt

Preparation Time: **10mins**

Ingredient List:

- 1 bay leaf
- 4 teaspoons each of fresh rosemary, oregano, basil, dill
- 4 teaspoons each of dried thyme, parsley, smoked paprika, ground mustard
- 4 teaspoons celery salt
- 4 teaspoons whole pink peppercorns
- 4 teaspoons white pepper
- 2 teaspoons granulated garlic
- 2 cups coarse sea salt

**Instructions:**

1. Add all ingredients to a food processor and pulse until you have a rough sandy texture.

2. Transfer the salt mix into pretty re-sealable jars!

# (40) Holly Cookies

Cute little cookies make the perfect gift, and what's more all the family and enjoy baking these festive treats.

Serving Size: **24**

Preparation Time: **35mins**

Ingredient List:

- 1 stick salted butter
- 30 large white mallows
- ½ teaspoons vanilla essence
- ½ teaspoons green food gel coloring
- 3½ cups cornflakes
- Red cinnamon candies

*Instructions:*

1. In a large pan or pot, melt the butter and mallows over moderate heat, while constantly stirring.

2. Add the vanilla essence along with the green gel. Add the cornflakes and stir to incorporate.

3. Using a lightly greased spoon, drop spoonfuls of the mixture onto a greased cookie tray.

4. Arrange 3 cinnamon candies on each sprig of holly, to look like red berries, and pressing them, so they adhere.

5. Allow the cookies to rest until they are set.

# Part 2

# Introduction

Welcome to the tenth volume of The Ultimate Christmas Recipes and Recipes For Christmas Collection!

There are various frosting recipes at the end of the book as well.

I hope you enjoy this cookbook and find some great recipes to use during the holiday season and throughout the year.

# Sugar Cut Out Cookies

Ingredients:

4 cups of flour

2 teaspoons of powder

1 teaspoon of salt

2 sticks of butter

1 ½ cups of sugar

2 eggs

2 teaspoons of vanilla extract

Directions:

Prepare the flour, baking powder and salt and sift into a large mixing bowl.

In a separate mixing bowl combine the butter and the sugar until creamy and smooth then mix the eggs and the vanilla. Slowly add the flour making the mixture into dough.

You can Refrigerate to chill the dough overnight to retain its firmness.

Preheat oven to 350 degrees.

Refrigerate the cookie dough for a minimum of two hours. If desired, you can prepare the sugar cookie dough and allow it to chill in the refrigerator overnight.

Knead the chilled cookie dough until it becomes pliable. Dust the ¼ cup of flour onto a clean, dry surface. Using a rolling pin, roll the cookie dough out until it is ¼ of an inch in thickness.

Use cookie cutters to cut the sugar cookies into your desired shapes. Place an 1 inch apart on the prepared cookie sheet.

Bake 7-9 minutes in the preheated oven. If you are using icing, candies or other products to decorate, let the cookies completely cool before beginning.

# Butter Cut Out Cookies

Ingredients

1 cup of butter softened

1 cup of sugar

1 fresh egg

1 teaspoon of vanilla extract

¼ cup of milk

3 cups of flour

1 teaspoon of baking powder

Directions

Combine sugar and butter in a large mixing bowl and beat with electric mixer until ingredients are creamed together. Stir in milk, egg and vanilla extract, set aside.

In a separate bowl combine baking soda and flour. Add dry mixture to wet mixture gradually mixing with electric mixer on low.

Refrigerate the cookie dough for a minimum of two hours. If desired, you can prepare the cookie dough and allow it to chill in the refrigerator overnight.

Preheat oven to 375 degrees.

Knead the chilled cookie dough until it becomes pliable. Dust the ¼ cup of flour onto a clean, dry surface. Using a rolling pin, roll the cookie dough out until it is ¼ of an inch in thickness.

Use cookie cutters to cut the sugar cookies into your desired shapes. Place an 1 inch apart on the prepared cookie sheet.

Bake 6 - 8 minutes in the preheated oven. If you are using icing, candies or other products to decorate, let the cookies completely cool before beginning.

# Chocolate Cut out Cookies

Ingredients

1 1/2 cups of flour

1 cup of unsweetened cocoa powder

1 ½ teaspoons of baking powder

½ teaspoon of salt

1 cup of butter, softened

1 ½ cups of sugar

1 egg

## Directions

In a mixing bowl sift together the baking powder, salt, cocoa and flour. Set aside.

Combine sugar and butter in a large mixing bowl and beat together. Stir in the vanilla extract and the egg.

Gradually add the dry mixture to the wet mixture, stir until a soft dough forms.

Refrigerate the cookie dough for a minimum of two hours. If desired, you can prepare the cookie dough and allow it to chill in the refrigerator overnight.

Preheat oven to 375 degrees.

Knead the chilled cookie dough until it becomes pliable. Dust the ¼ cup of flour onto a clean, dry surface. Using a rolling pin, roll the cookie dough out until it is ¼ of an inch in thickness.

Use cookie cutters to cut the sugar cookies into your desired shapes. Place an 1 inch apart on the prepared cookie sheet.

Bake 7-*9 minutes in the preheated oven*. If you are using icing, candies or other products to decorate, let the cookies completely cool before beginning.

# Gingerbread Cut Out Cookies

An appetizer which will surprisingly add the zing taste of a spicy ginger in cookie dough with the bits of a black pepper and cinnamon twist

Ingredients

1 cup of sugar

1 cup of butter, softened

1 egg

1 cup of dark molasses

2 tablespoons of vinegar

4 ½ cups of flour

1 ½ teaspoons of baking soda

1 teaspoon of salt

2 teaspoons of vanilla extract

1 teaspoon of ginger

1 teaspoon of cloves

1 ½ teaspoons of cinnamon

Directions

Sift together dry ingredients into a mixing bowl and set aside.

In a separate mixing bowl beat sugar and butter until creamy.

Beat in vinegar, molasses and the egg. Gradually add the dry ingredients into the wet ingredients.

Refrigerate the cookie dough for a minimum of two hours. If desired, you can prepare the cookie dough and allow it to chill *in the refrigerator overnight.*

Preheat oven to 375 degrees.

Knead the chilled cookie dough until it becomes pliable. Dust the ¼ cup of flour onto a clean, dry surface. Using a rolling pin, roll the cookie dough out until it is ¼ of an inch in thickness.

Use cookie cutters to cut the sugar cookies into your desired shapes. Place an 1 inch apart on the prepared cookie sheet.

Bake 7-*9 minutes in the preheated oven*. If you are using icing, candies or other products to decorate, let the cookies completely cool before beginning.

# Soft Cut Out Cookies

Ingredients:

4 cups of flour

1 teaspoon of baking powder

1 teaspoon of salt

1 cup of butter, softened

1 ½ cups of sugar

2 eggs

2 ½ teaspoons of vanilla extract

Directions:

In a mixing bowl, sift together salt, baking powder and flour. Set aside.

In a large mixing bowl cream together sugar and butter. Beat in the vanilla and then the eggs, one at a time.

Gradually blend in the dry ingredients until well combined.

Refrigerate the cookie dough for a minimum of two hours. If desired, you can prepare the cookie dough and allow it to chill ***in the refrigerator overnight.***

Preheat oven to 375 degrees.

Knead the chilled cookie dough until it becomes pliable. Dust the ¼ cup of flour onto a clean, dry surface. Using a rolling pin, roll the cookie dough out until it is ¼ of an inch in thickness.

Use cookie cutters to cut the sugar cookies into your desired shapes. Place an 1 inch apart on the prepared cookie sheet.

Bake 7-*9 minutes in the preheated oven*. If you are using icing, candies or other products to decorate, let the cookies completely cool before beginning.

# Cream Cheese Cut Out Cookies

Ingredients:

1 cup of softened butter

4 ounces of cream cheese, softened

1 cup of sugar

½ teaspoon of salt

1 egg

2 ¾ cups of flour

2 teaspoons of vanilla extract

Directions

Cream together sugar, salt, butter and cream cheese. Beat in vanilla and egg. Gradually mix in flour.

Refrigerate the cookie dough for a minimum of two hours. If desired, you can prepare the cookie dough and allow it to chill in the refrigerator overnight.

Preheat oven to 375 degrees.

Knead the chilled cookie dough until it becomes pliable. Dust the ¼ cup of flour onto a clean, dry surface. Using a rolling pin, roll the cookie dough out until it is ¼ of an inch in thickness.

Use cookie cutters to cut the sugar cookies into your desired shapes. Place an 1 inch apart on the prepared cookie sheet.

Bake 7-9 minutes in the preheated oven. If you are using icing, candies or other products to decorate, let the cookies completely cool before beginning.

# Shortbread Cut Out Cookies

Ingredients:

2 cups of butter, softened
½ cups of confectioners' sugar
2 1/2 tablespoons of vanilla extract
2 teaspoons of baking powder
4 ½ cups of flour

Directions:

Cream together the sugar and butter. Mix in egg and vanilla. Gradually add baking powder and flour into wet mixture at low speed until combined.

Refrigerate the cookie dough for a minimum of two hours. If desired, you can prepare the cookie dough and allow it to chill in the refrigerator overnight.

Preheat oven to 350 degrees.

Knead the chilled cookie dough until it becomes pliable. Dust the ¼ cup of flour onto a clean, dry surface. Using a rolling pin, roll the cookie dough out until it is ¼ of an inch in thickness.

Use cookie cutters to cut the sugar cookies into your desired shapes. Place an 1 inch apart on the prepared cookie sheet.

Bake 10 - 12 minutes in the preheated oven. If you are using icing, candies or other products to decorate, let the cookies completely cool before beginning.

## Anise Cut Out Cookies Ingredients

Ingredients:

1 cup of sugar

2 cups of shortening

2 eggs

2 ½ teaspoons of aniseed

5 ½ cups of flour

1 teaspoon of salt

¼ cup of apple juice

Directions

Cream sugar and shortening until light and fluffy. Mix in aniseed and eggs. Gradually add the baking powder, salt and flour into wet mixture. Stir in apple juice and mix together well.

Refrigerate the cookie dough for a minimum of two hours. If desired, you can prepare the cookie dough and allow it to chill in the refrigerator overnight.

Preheat oven to 375 degrees.

Knead the chilled cookie dough until it becomes pliable. Dust the ¼ cup of flour onto a clean, dry surface. Using a rolling pin, roll the cookie dough out until it is ¼ of an inch in thickness.

Use cookie cutters to cut the cookies into your desired shapes. Place an 1 inch apart on the prepared cookie sheet.

Bake for 13 – 15 minutes in the preheated oven. If you are using icing, candies or other products to decorate, let the cookies completely cool before beginning.

# Vanilla Cut Out Cookies

Ingredients:

2 cups of flour
½ teaspoon of baking powder
½ teaspoon of salt
¾ cup of butter, softened
1 cup of sugar
1 egg
1 ½ teaspoon of vanilla extract

Directions:

In a medium sized mixing bowl, combine salt, baking powder and flour.

In a large mixing bowl cream together the sugar and the butter until light and fluffy. Mix in vanilla and egg. Turn the mixer to low and gradually add the dry mixture to the wet mixture.

Refrigerate the cookie dough for a minimum of two hours. If desired, you can prepare the cookie dough and allow it to chill in the refrigerator overnight.

Preheat to 350 degrees.

Knead the chilled cookie dough until it becomes pliable. Dust the ¼ cup of flour onto a clean, dry surface. Using a rolling pin, roll the cookie dough out until it is ¼ of an inch in thickness.

Use cookie cutters to cut the cookies into your desired shapes. Place an 1 inch apart on the prepared cookie sheet.

Bake 10 - 12 minutes in the preheated oven. If you are using icing, candies or other products to decorate, let the cookies completely cool before beginning.

# Chocolate Spice Cut Out Cookies

Ingredients:

2/3 cup of shortening
½ cup of sugar
1 teaspoon on baking soda
1 teaspoon of ginger
1 teaspoon of baking powder
½ teaspoon of clovers
1 teaspoon of cinnamon
½ cup of dark corn syrup
1 egg
3 cups of flour
½ cup of unsweetened cocoa powder

Directions:

In a large mixing bowl cream together sugar and shortening. Beat in baking soda, baking powder, cinnamon, ginger and cloves until well combined.
Add corn syrup, milk and egg and beat again.
In a separate bowl combine cocoa powder and flour and mix well. Gradually beat dry ingredients into wet ingredients.
Refrigerate the cookie dough for a minimum of two hours. If desired, you can prepare the cookie dough and allow it to chill in the refrigerator overnight.

Preheat oven to 375 degrees.

Knead the chilled cookie dough until it becomes pliable. Dust the ¼ cup of flour onto a clean, dry surface. Using a rolling pin, roll the cookie dough out until it is ¼ of an inch in thickness.

Use cookie cutters to cut the sugar cookies into your desired shapes. Place an 1 inch apart on the prepared cookie sheet.

Bake 6 - 8 minutes in the preheated oven. If you are using icing, candies or other products to decorate, let the cookies completely cool before beginning.

# Almond Shortbread Cut Out Cookies

Ingredients:

1 cup of butter
¾ cup of powdered sugar
1 teaspoon of vanilla
½ teaspoon of almond extract
1 teaspoon of cinnamon
¼ teaspoon of ginger
¼ teaspoon of salt
1 cut of blanched almonds, ground
2 ½ cups of flour

Directions:

Combine dry ingredient in a bowl, set aside.
Cream together butter and powdered sugar until light and fluffy.
Stir in vanilla extract and almond extract.
Gradually add dry ingredients to wet ingredients.
Refrigerate the cookie dough for a minimum of two hours. If desired, you can prepare the cookie dough and allow it to chill in the refrigerator overnight.
Preheat oven to 350 degrees.

 Knead the chilled cookie dough until it becomes pliable. Dust the ¼ cup of flour onto a clean, dry surface. Using a rolling pin, roll the cookie dough out until it is ¼ of an inch in thickness.

Use cookie cutters to cut the sugar cookies into your desired shapes. Place an 1 inch apart on the prepared cookie sheet.
Bake 9 - 11 minutes in the preheated oven. If you are using icing, candies or other products to decorate, let the cookies completely cool before beginning.

# Chocolate Shortbread Cookies

Ingredients:

½ pound of butter, softened
1 cup of powdered sugar
2/3 cup of unsweetened cocoa powder
1 teaspoon of vanilla extract
1 ½ cups of flour
½ teaspoon of salt
½ teaspoon of baking powder

Directions:

In a mixing bowl combine flour, baking powder, salt and cocoa. Set aside.

In a separate bowl, Cream together powdered sugar and butter. Mix in vanilla.

Gradually mix dry ingredients into wet ingredients.
Refrigerate the cookie dough for a minimum of two hours. If desired, you can prepare the cookie dough and allow it to chill *in the refrigerator overnight.*

 Preheat oven to 350 degrees.
Knead the chilled cookie dough until it becomes pliable. Dust the ¼ cup of flour onto a clean, dry surface. Using a rolling pin, roll the cookie dough out until it is ¼ of an inch in thickness.

Use cookie cutters to cut the cookies into your desired shapes. Place an 1 inch apart on the prepared cookie sheet.

Bake *11 - 13 minutes in the preheated oven*. If you are using icing, candies or other products to decorate, let the cookies completely cool before beginning.

# Apple Cinnamon Cut Out Cookies

Ingredients:

3 cups of flour
1 ½ teaspoons of salt
1 ½ teaspoons of baking powder
1 teaspoon of cinnamon
1 cup of butter, softened
¾ cup of brown sugar
1 egg
3 tablespoons of apple juice concentrated, room temp

Directions:

In a medium mixing bowl combine baking powder, salt, cinnamon and the flour. Set aside.
In another bowl, cream together the sugar and the butter, mix until light and fluffy.
Stir in the apple juice concentrate and the egg, mix until new ingredients are well blended.
Gradually add the dry mixture to the wet mixture.
Refrigerate the cookie dough for a minimum of two hours. If desired, you can prepare the cookie dough and allow it to chill in the refrigerator overnight.

Preheat oven to 350 degrees.
Knead the chilled cookie dough until it becomes pliable. Dust the ¼ cup of flour onto a clean, dry surface. Using a rolling pin, roll the cookie dough out until it is ¼ of an inch in thickness.

Use cookie cutters to cut the cookies into your desired shapes. Place an 1 inch apart on the prepared cookie sheet.

Bake 8 - 10 minutes in the preheated oven. If you are using icing, candies or other products to decorate, let the cookies completely cool before beginning.

# Simple Scottish Shortbread Cut Out Cookies

Ingredients:

2 cups of butter
1 cup of brown sugar
3 ½ cups of flour

Directions:

Cream brown sugar and butter together. Gradually add flour to mixture. Mix well.

Refrigerate the cookie dough for a minimum of two hours. If desired, you can prepare the cookie dough and allow it to chill in the refrigerator overnight.

Preheat oven to 350 degrees.
Knead the chilled cookie dough until it becomes pliable. Dust the ¼ cup of flour onto a clean, dry surface. Using a rolling pin, roll the cookie dough out until it is ¼ of an inch in thickness.
Use cookie cutters to cut the sugar cookies into your desired shapes. Place an 1 inch apart on the prepared cookie sheet.
Bake 18 - 20 minutes in the preheated oven. If you are using icing, candies or other products to decorate, let the cookies completely cool before beginning.

# German Cut Out Cookies

Ingredients:

1 cup of butter, softened
2/3 cup of sugar
½ cup of light corn syrup
1 tablespoon of lemon juice
1 egg, beaten
4 cups of flour
½ teaspoon of salt

Directions:

Cream sugar and butter until light and fluffy. Mix in lemon juice, egg and light corn syrup.
In a separate mixing bowl, combine salt and flour. Gradually add dry mixture to wet mixture.
Refrigerate the cookie dough for a minimum of two hours. If desired, you can prepare the cookie dough and allow it to chill in the refrigerator overnight.

 Preheat oven to 350 degrees.
Knead the chilled cookie dough until it becomes pliable. Dust the ¼ cup of flour onto a clean, dry surface. Using a rolling pin, roll the cookie dough out until it is ¼ of an inch in thickness.
Use cookie cutters to cut the cookies into your desired shapes. Place an 1 inch apart on the prepared cookie sheet.

Bake 10 - 12 minutes in the preheated oven. If you are using icing, candies or other products to decorate, let the cookies completely cool before beginning.

# Pumpkin Cut Out Cookies

Ingredients:

¾ cup of butter
½ cup of brown sugar
1 tablespoon of orange zest
½ cup o pumpkin puree
1 egg
1 ½ teaspoons of vanilla extract
½ teaspoon of ground cinnamon
½ teaspoon of ground nutmeg
½ teaspoon of ground ginger
¼ teaspoon of salt
2 ½ cups of flour

Directions:

Sift together salt, ginger, cinnamon, nutmeg and flour. Set aside. In a medium mixing bowl cream together the orange zest, brown sugar and butter. Stir in the vanilla, egg and pumpkin and mix well.

Gradually add the dry ingredients to the wet ingredients.

Refrigerate the cookie dough for a minimum of two hours. If desired, you can prepare the cookie dough and allow it to chill in the refrigerator overnight.

Preheat oven to 375 degrees.

Knead the chilled cookie dough until it becomes pliable. Dust the ¼ cup of flour onto a clean, dry surface. Using a rolling pin, roll the cookie dough out until it is ¼ of an inch in thickness.

Use cookie cutters to cut the cookies into your desired shapes. Place an 1 inch apart on the prepared cookie sheet.

Bake 10 – 12 minutes in the preheated oven. If you are using icing, candies or other products to decorate, let the cookies completely cool before beginning.

# Cinnamon Cut Out Cookies

Ingredients:

2 cups of flour
¾ cup of butter
1 ½ cups of sugar
2 eggs
2 teaspoons of cinnamon
1 ½ teaspoon of baking powder
1 teaspoon of salt

Directions:

Cream together sugar and butter. Beat in eggs, one at a time.
In a separate bowl combine dry ingredients. Gradually add dry mixture to wet mixture, combine well.
Refrigerate the cookie dough for a minimum of two hours. If desired, you can prepare the cookie dough and allow it to chill in the refrigerator overnight.

 Preheat oven to 350 degrees.
Knead the chilled cookie dough until it becomes pliable. Dust the ¼ cup of flour onto a clean, dry surface. Using a rolling pin, roll the cookie dough out until it is ¼ of an inch in thickness.
Use cookie cutters to cut the cookies into your desired shapes. Place an 1 inch apart on the prepared cookie sheet.

Bake 9 - 11 minutes in the preheated oven. If you are using icing, candies or other products to decorate, let the cookies completely cool before beginning.

# Sour Cream Cut Out Cookies

Ingredients:

1 cup of butter, softened
1 ½ cups of sugar
2 eggs
1 ½ teaspoons of vanilla extract
½ teaspoon of salt
1 teaspoon of baking soda
1 teaspoon of baking powder
1 cup of sour cream, room temp
4 ½ cups of flour
Directions:

In a large mixing bowl beat together vanilla, sour cream, eggs, sugar and butter. Gradually add dry ingredients to the mixture. Refrigerate the cookie dough for a minimum of two hours. If desired, you can prepare the cookie dough and allow it to chill in the refrigerator overnight.

 Preheat oven to 350 degrees.
Knead the chilled cookie dough until it becomes pliable. Dust the ¼ cup of flour onto a clean, dry surface. Using a rolling pin, roll the cookie dough out until it is ¼ of an inch in thickness.
Use cookie cutters to cut the cookies into your desired shapes. Place an 1 inch apart on the prepared cookie sheet.

Bake 9 - 11 minutes in the preheated oven. If you are using icing, candies or other products to decorate, let the cookies completely cool before beginning.

# Crispy Cornmeal Cut Out Cookies

Ingredients:

1 cup of butter, softened

1 cup of sugar

2 eggs

1 teaspoon of vanilla extract

1 teaspoon of orange extract

1 teaspoon of orange zest

1 ½ cups of flour

1 cup of cornmeal

1 teaspoon of salt

½ teaspoon of nutmeg

½ teaspoon of cinnamon

Directions:

Cream together butter and sugar until fluffy. Mix in orange extract, vanilla extract, orange zest and eggs.

In a separate bowl combine the salt, cinnamon, nutmeg, flour and cornmeal. Gradually mix dry ingredients into wet ingredients.

Refrigerate the cookie dough for a minimum of two hours. If desired, you can prepare the cookie dough and allow it to chill in the refrigerator overnight.

Preheat oven to 350 degrees.

Knead the chilled cookie dough until it becomes pliable. Dust the ¼ cup of flour onto a clean, dry surface. Using a rolling pin, roll the cookie dough out until it is ¼ of an inch in thickness.

Use cookie cutters to cut the cookies into your desired shapes. Place an 1 inch apart on the prepared cookie sheet.

Bake 7-9 minutes in the preheated oven. If you are using icing, candies or other products to decorate, let the cookies completely cool before beginning.

# Brown Sugar Shortbread Cookies

Ingredients:

1 cut of butter, softened

1 ½ cups of brown sugar

1 ½ teaspoons of vanilla extract

2 ½ cups of flour

Directions:

Preheat oven to 325 degrees.

Beat together sugar and butter in a large mixing bowl until creamy. Add vanilla. Gradually beat in the flour, ½ cup at a time until well combined.

Refrigerate the cookie dough for a minimum of two hours. If desired, you can prepare the cookie dough and allow it to chill *in the refrigerator overnight.*

Knead the chilled cookie dough until it becomes pliable. Dust the ¼ cup of flour onto a clean, dry surface. Using a rolling pin, roll the cookie dough out until it is ¼ of an inch in thickness.

Use cookie cutters to cut the sugar cookies into your desired shapes. Place an 1 inch apart on the prepared cookie sheet.

Bake 30 - 35 *minutes in the preheated oven*. If you are using icing, candies or other products to decorate, let the cookies completely cool before beginning.

# Oat Flour Cut Out Cookies

Ingredients:

1 ½ cups of powdered sugar
1 cup of butter, softened
1 egg
1 ½ teaspoons of vanilla extract
2 ½ cups of flour
1 cup of oat flour
1 teaspoon of baking soda

Directions:

Cream together the butter and powdered sugar in a large mixing bowl. Beat in the vanilla and the egg.
In a separate bowl, combine the baking soda, flour and oat flour. Gradually add the flour mixture into the wet mixture until well combined.
Preheat oven to 375 degrees.

Refrigerate the cookie dough for a minimum of two hours. If desired, you can prepare the cookie dough and allow it to chill in the refrigerator overnight.
Knead the chilled cookie dough until it becomes pliable. Dust the ¼ cup of flour onto a clean, dry surface. Using a rolling pin, roll the cookie dough out until it is ¼ of an inch in thickness.

Use cookie cutters to cut the cookies into your desired shapes. Place 2 inches apart on the prepared cookie sheet.

Bake 7-8 minutes in the preheated oven. If you are using icing, candies or other products to decorate, let the cookies completely cool before beginning.

# Whole Wheat Cut Out Cookies

Ingredients:

4 cups of whole wheat flour
1 cup of butter, softened
1 cup of honey
1 egg, beaten
½ cup of hot water
2 tablespoons of baking powder

Directions:

Mix together water, egg, honey and butter in a large mixing bowl. Add baking powder and whole wheat flour to the wet mixture until well combined.

Preheat oven to 350 degrees.

Refrigerate the cookie dough for a minimum of two hours. If desired, you can prepare the cookie dough and allow it to chill in the refrigerator overnight.

Knead the chilled cookie dough until it becomes pliable. Dust the ¼ cup of flour onto a clean, dry surface. Using a rolling pin, roll the cookie dough out until it is ¼ of an inch in thickness.

Use cookie cutters to cut the sugar cookies into your desired shapes. Place an 1 inch apart on the prepared cookie sheet.

Bake 12 - 15 minutes in the preheated oven. If you are using icing, candies or other products to decorate, let the cookies completely cool before beginning.

## Soft Gingerbread Cookies

Ingredients:

¾ cup of molasses
1/3 cup of brown sugar
1 /4 cup of butter, softened
3 ½ cups of flour
1/3 cup o water
1 teaspoon of baking soda
½ teaspoon of allspice, ground
1 teaspoon of ginger, ground
½ teaspoon of cloves, ground
1 teaspoon of cinnamon, ground

Directions:

Mix together water, butter, brown sugar and the molasses in a medium sized mixing bowl until smooth.

In a separate bowl combine the cinnamon, cloves, ginger, allspice, baking soda and flour together. Gradually stir the dry mixture into the wet mixture.

Preheat oven to 350 degrees.

Refrigerate the cookie dough for a minimum of two hours. If desired, you can prepare the cookie dough and allow it to chill in the refrigerator overnight.

Knead the chilled cookie dough until it becomes pliable. Dust the ¼ cup of flour onto a clean, dry surface. Using a rolling pin, roll the cookie dough out until it is ¼ of an inch in thickness.

Use cookie cutters to cut the cookies into your desired shapes. Place an 1 inch apart on the prepared cookie sheet.

Bake 8 - 10 minutes in the preheated oven. If you are using icing, candies or other products to decorate, let the cookies completely cool before beginning.

# Pumpkin Gingerbread Cut Out Cookies

Ingredients:

3 cups of flour
1 teaspoon of baking powder
½ teaspoon of salt
1 cup of sugar
½ cup of butter, softened
¼ cup of molasses
1 egg
¼ cup of pumpkin puree
3 teaspoons of pumpkin pie spice
1 ½ teaspoons of vanilla extract

Directions:

Sift together salt, baking powder and flour in a medium sized mixing bowl.
In a large mixing bowl cream together the sugar and the butter until well blended. Beat in the pumpkin puree, molasses, spices, egg and vanilla extract. Gradually stir in the flour mixture.
Preheat oven to 375 degrees.
Refrigerate the cookie dough for a minimum of two hours. If desired, you can prepare the cookie dough and allow it to chill *in the refrigerator overnight.*
Knead the chilled cookie dough until it becomes pliable. Dust the ¼ cup of flour onto a clean, dry surface. Using a rolling pin, roll the cookie dough out until it is ¼ of an inch in thickness.

Use cookie cutters to cut the sugar cookies into your desired shapes. Place an 1 inch apart on the prepared cookie sheet.

Bake 7-*9 minutes in the preheated oven*. If you are using icing, candies or other products to decorate, let the cookies completely cool before beginning.

# Chocolate Brownie Cut Out Cookies

Ingredients:

3 cups of flour
1 teaspoon of salt
1 teaspoon of baking powder
1 cut of butter, softened
1 ½ cups of sugar
2 eggs
1 ½ teaspoons of vanilla extract
2/3 cup of unsweetened cocoa powder

Directions:

Sift together salt, baking powder and flour. Set aside.
Mix together sugar and butter. Add eggs and vanilla. Finally beat in cocoa. Gradually add flour mixture.
Refrigerate the cookie dough for a minimum of two hours. If desired, you can prepare the cookie dough and allow it to chill in the refrigerator overnight.
Preheat oven to 350 degrees.
Knead the chilled cookie dough until it becomes pliable. Dust the ¼ cup of flour onto a clean, dry surface. Using a rolling pin, roll the cookie dough out until it is ¼ of an inch in thickness.

Use cookie cutters to cut the cookies into your desired shapes. Place an 1 inch apart on the prepared cookie sheet.

Bake 9 - 11 minutes in the preheated oven. If you are using icing, candies or other products to decorate, let the cookies completely cool before beginning.

# Chocolate Cherry Cut Out Cookies

Ingredients:

1 cup of flour
1/3 cup of unsweetened cocoa powder
1 teaspoon of baking powder
½ teaspoon of salt
1 cup of sugar
½ cup of butter, softened
1 teaspoon of vanilla extract
1 egg
2/3 cup of dried cherries
4 tablespoons of milk chocolate chips

Directions:

In a large bowl combine baking soda, baking powder, salt, cocoa and flour. Set aside.

Cream butter and sugar together in a large bowl until well blended. Add egg and vanilla. Gradually add flour mixture. Fold in cherries and Chocolate Chips.

Refrigerate the cookie dough for a minimum of two hours. If desired, you can prepare the cookie dough and allow it to chill ***in the refrigerator overnight.***

Preheat oven to 350 degrees.

Knead the chilled cookie dough until it becomes pliable. Dust the ¼ cup of flour onto a clean, dry surface. Using a rolling pin, roll the cookie dough out until it is ¼ of an inch in thickness.

Use cookie cutters to cut the cookies into your desired shapes. Place an 1 inch apart on the prepared cookie sheet.

Bake 11 - 13 ***minutes in the preheated oven***. If you are using icing, candies or other products to decorate, let the cookies completely cool before beginning.

# Dark Chocolate Cut Out Sugar Cookies

Ingredients:

6 cups of flour
1 ½ cups of dark cocoa powder
1 ½ teaspoons of salt
2 cups of butter, softened
2 cups of sugar
1 cup of brown sugar
3 eggs
2 ½ teaspoons of vanilla extract

Directions:

Sift together salt, cocoa powder and flour in a large bowl. Set aside.
In another large bowl, cream together sugar, brown sugar and butter until creamy. Beat in eggs and vanilla.

Gradually add dry mixture into wet mixture until combined.
Refrigerate the cookie dough for a minimum of two hours. If desired, you can prepare the cookie dough and allow it to chill in the refrigerator overnight.

Preheat oven to 325 degrees.
Knead the chilled cookie dough until it becomes pliable. Dust the ¼ cup of flour onto a clean, dry surface. Using a rolling pin, roll the cookie dough out until it is ¼ of an inch in thickness.

Use cookie cutters to cut the cookies into your desired shapes. Place an 1 inch apart on the prepared cookie sheet.

Bake 14 - 16 minutes in the preheated oven. If you are using icing, candies or other products to decorate, let the cookies completely cool before beginning.

# Orange Chocolate Cut Out Cookies

Ingredients:

½ cup of butter, softened
¾ cup of sugar
1 egg
1 ½ teaspoons of vanilla extract
1 ½ cups of flour
6 tablespoons of unsweetened cocoa powder
1 teaspoon of baking powder
½ teaspoon of salt
4 tablespoons of orange extract

Directions:

In a large bowl, combine baking powder, salt, cocoa and flour. Set aside.

In another large mixing bowl cream the sugar and butter together. Add the vanilla and the egg and beat well. Add the orange extract and beat until well combined.

Gradually add the dry mixture the the wet mixture.

Refrigerate the cookie dough for a minimum of two hours. If desired, you can prepare the cookie dough and allow it to chill in the refrigerator overnight.

Preheat oven to 325 degrees.

Knead the chilled cookie dough until it becomes pliable. Dust the ¼ cup of flour onto a clean, dry surface. Using a rolling pin, roll the cookie dough out until it is ¼ of an inch in thickness.

Use cookie cutters to cut the cookies into your desired shapes. Place an 1 inch apart on the prepared cookie sheet.

Bake 8 - 10 minutes in the preheated oven. If you are using icing, candies or other products to decorate, let the cookies completely cool before beginning.

NOTE:

This recipe will make the orange chocolate flavor very strong. If you only want a hint of orange chocolate, try it with only 2 tablespoons of orange extract.

# White Chocolate Cut Out Cookies

Ingredients:

1 cup of butter

4 ounces of white chocolate

2 cups of sugar

2 eggs

½ teaspoon of cream of tartar

1 teaspoon of baking soda

1 teaspoon of salt

3 cups of flour

Directions:

Place butter and white chocolate in a large microwave safe bowl and heat until the chocolate has begun to melt. Take out of microwave and stir until melting is completed.

Stir in the sugar and beat until it is completely dissolved. Beat in the eggs one at a time.

In a separate bowl combine the salt, baking soda, cream of tartar and flour. Gradually mix the dry ingredients into the wet ingredients.

Refrigerate the cookie dough for a minimum of two hours. If desired, you can prepare the cookie dough and allow it to chill in the refrigerator overnight.

Preheat oven to 375 degrees.

Knead the chilled cookie dough until it becomes pliable. Dust the ¼ cup of flour onto a clean, dry surface. Using a rolling pin, roll the cookie dough out until it is ¼ of an inch in thickness.

Use cookie cutters to cut the cookies into your desired shapes. Place an 1 inch apart on the prepared cookie sheet.

Bake 7-9 minutes in the preheated oven. If you are using icing, candies or other products to decorate, let the cookies completely cool before beginning.

# Molasses Cut Out Cookies

Ingredients:

1 cup of shortening
½ cup of sugar
½ cup of brown sugar
2 eggs
1 cup of dark molasses
5 ½ cups of flour
1 teaspoon of baking soda
1 teaspoon of baking powder
1 teaspoon of ginger, ground
1 ½ teaspoon of cinnamon, ground
1 teaspoon of salt
½ cup of water

Directions:

In a medium sized mixing bowl combine the ginger, cinnamon, salt, baking soda, baking powder and flour. Set aside.

In another mixing bowl cream together the sugar, brown sugar and butter until light and fluffy. Add the eggs, beating them into the batter one at a time. Gradually add the dry mixture to the wet mixture until well combined.

Refrigerate the cookie dough for a minimum of two hours. If desired, you can prepare the cookie dough and allow it to chill *in the refrigerator overnight.*

Preheat oven to 350 degrees.

Knead the chilled cookie dough until it becomes pliable. Dust the ¼ cup of flour onto a clean, dry surface. Using a rolling pin, roll the cookie dough out until it is ¼ of an inch in thickness.

Use cookie cutters to cut the cookies into your desired shapes. Place an 1 inch apart on the prepared cookie sheet.

Bake 8 - 10 *minutes in the preheated oven*. If you are using icing, candies or other products to decorate, let the cookies completely cool before beginning.

# Orange Cut Out Sugar Cookies

Ingredients:

2 ½ cups of flour
1 teaspoon o baking powder
½ teaspoon of salt
¾ cup of butter, softened
¾ cup of sugar
2 eggs
2 tablespoons of orange juice
1 ½ tablespoons of orange extract

Directions:

Combine the baking powder, salt and flour in a medium sized mixing bowl. Set aside.

Cream the sugar and butter in a large mixing bowl. Beat in the eggs, one at a time. Add the orange juice and orange extract and beat until combined.

Gradually add the flour mixture to the wet mixture until well combined.

Refrigerate the cookie dough for a minimum of two hours. If desired, you can prepare the cookie dough and allow it to chill in the refrigerator overnight.

Preheat oven to 350 degrees.

Knead the chilled cookie dough until it becomes pliable. Dust the ¼ cup of flour onto a clean, dry surface. Using a rolling pin, roll the cookie dough out until it is ¼ of an inch in thickness.

Use cookie cutters to cut the cookies into your desired shapes. Place an 1 inch apart on the prepared cookie sheet.

Bake 9 - 11 minutes in the preheated oven. If you are using icing, candies or other products to decorate, let the cookies completely cool before beginning.

# Orange Butter Cut Out Cookies

Ingredients:

2 ½ cups of flour
1 teaspoon of salt
¼ teaspoon of baking powder
1 cup of butter, salted
1 cup of sugar
2 tablespoons of orange zest, finely grated
2 eggs
1 teaspoon of vanilla extract
1 tablespoon of orange extract

Directions:

Combine the salt, baking powder and flour in a medium mixing bowl.
In a large mixing bowl, cream together the sugar and butter until light and fluffy. Mix in the orange zest, the orange extract and the vanilla extract. Beat in the eggs, one at a time.
Gradually add the dry ingredients to the wet ingredients.
Refrigerate the cookie dough for a minimum of two hours. If desired, you can prepare the cookie dough and allow it to chill in the refrigerator overnight.
Preheat oven to 350 degrees.
Knead the chilled cookie dough until it becomes pliable. Dust the ¼ cup of flour onto a clean, dry surface. Using a rolling pin, roll the cookie dough out until it is ¼ of an inch in thickness.

Use cookie cutters to cut the cookies into your desired shapes. Place an 1 inch apart on the prepared cookie sheet.

Bake 10 - 12 minutes in the preheated oven. If you are using icing, candies or other products to decorate, let the cookies completely cool before beginning.

# Chocolate Raspberry Cut Out Cookies

Ingredients:

1 cup of butter, softened
1 cup of sugar
1 egg
1 egg yolk
2 ½ teaspoons of vanilla extract
2 ½ cups of flour
½ cup of baking cocoa powder
1 teaspoon of salt
½ teaspoon of baking powder
½ teaspoon of cinnamon, ground
1 ½ tablespoons of raspberry extract

Directions:

Combine salt, baking powder, cinnamon, cocoa and flour in bowl, mix well.

Cream together sugar and butter in a large mixing bowl until light and fluffy. Beat in the egg yolk, the whole egg, the vanilla extract and the raspberry extract.

Gradually add the dry mixture to the wet mixture and mix together well.

Refrigerate the cookie dough for a minimum of two hours. If desired, you can prepare the cookie dough and allow it to chill *in the refrigerator overnight.*

Preheat oven to 375 degrees.

Knead the chilled cookie dough until it becomes pliable. Dust the ¼ cup of flour onto a clean, dry surface. Using a rolling pin, roll the cookie dough out until it is ¼ of an inch in thickness.

Use cookie cutters to cut the cookies into your desired shapes. Place an 1 inch apart on the prepared cookie sheet.

Bake 6 - 8 ***minutes in the preheated oven***. If you are using icing, candies or other products to decorate, let the cookies completely cool before beginning.

# Ginger Spice Cut Out Cookies

Ingredients:

½ cup of butter, softened
½ cup of brown sugar
¼ cup of molasses
1 ½ teaspoon of vanilla extract
1 egg
2 cups of flour
1 teaspoon of ginger, ground
½ teaspoon of baking powder
½ teaspoon of cinnamon, ground
½ teaspoon of salt
¼ teaspoon o nutmeg, ground

Directions:

Combine flour, ginger, cinnamon, nutmeg, salt and baking powder in a medium bowl and mix together well. Set aside.
In a large mixing bowl cream together the sugar, sugar and the molasses. Beat in the egg and vanilla extract.
Gradually beat in the dry ingredients into the wet ingredients.
Refrigerate the cookie dough for a minimum of two hours. If desired, you can prepare the cookie dough and allow it to chill *in the refrigerator overnight.*
Preheat oven to 350 degrees.

Knead the chilled cookie dough until it becomes pliable. Dust the ¼ cup of flour onto a clean, dry surface. Using a rolling pin, roll the cookie dough out until it is ¼ of an inch in thickness.

Use cookie cutters to cut the cookies into your desired shapes. Place an 1 inch apart on the prepared cookie sheet.

Bake 10 - 12 ***minutes in the preheated oven***. If you are using icing, candies or other products to decorate, let the cookies completely cool before beginning.

# Chocolate Coconut Cut Out Cookies

Ingredients:

1 cup of butter
1 ½ cups of confectioners' sugar
½ cup of baking cocoa powder
1 egg
1 teaspoon of coconut extract
1 teaspoon of vanilla extract
3 cups of flour
1 teaspoon of baking powder
1 teaspoon of salt
1 cup of coconut flakes.

Directions:

In a medium bowl mix together flour, baking cocoa, baking powder and salt. Set aside.

In a large mixing bowl, cream together the sugar and the butter until light and fluffy. Beat in the egg, the coconut extract and the vanilla extract. Stir in the coconut flakes.

Gradually add the dry ingredients into the wet ingredients.

Refrigerate the cookie dough for a minimum of two hours. If desired, you can prepare the cookie dough and allow it to chill ***in the refrigerator overnight.***

Preheat oven to 350 degrees.

Knead the chilled cookie dough until it becomes pliable. Dust the ¼ cup of flour onto a clean, dry surface. Using a rolling pin, roll the cookie dough out until it is ¼ of an inch in thickness.

Use cookie cutters to cut the cookies into your desired shapes. Place an 1 inch apart on the prepared cookie sheet.

Bake 8 - 10 **minutes in the preheated oven**. If you are using icing, candies or other products to decorate, let the cookies completely cool before beginning.

# Lemon Shortbread Cut Out Cookies

Ingredients:

2 cups of flour
¼ cup of cornstarch
½ teaspoon of salt
1 cup of butter, softened
½ cup of confectioners' sugar
1 teaspoon of vanilla extract
1 tablespoon of lemon zest
1 tablespoon of lemon juice

Directions:

In a medium sized mixing bowl sift together cornstarch, salt and flour. Set aside.

In a large mixing bowl beat together sugar and butter until light and fluffy. Mix in lemon zest, lemon juice and vanilla extract.

Gradually add the dry mixture to the wet mixture until well combined.

Refrigerate the cookie dough for a minimum of two hours. If desired, you can prepare the cookie dough and allow it to chill *in the refrigerator overnight.*

Preheat oven to 350 degrees.

Knead the chilled cookie dough until it becomes pliable. Dust the ¼ cup of flour onto a clean, dry surface. Using a rolling pin, roll the cookie dough out until it is ¼ of an inch in thickness.

Use cookie cutters to cut the cookies into your desired shapes. Place an 1 inch apart on the prepared cookie sheet.

Bake 10 - 12 ***minutes in the preheated oven***. If you are using icing, candies or other products to decorate, let the cookies completely cool before beginning.

# Banana Cut Out Cookies

Ingredients:

1 cup of butter
1 ½ cups of powdered sugar
1 egg
1 tablespoon of banana extract
1 ½ teaspoons of vanilla extract
3 cups of flour
1 ½ teaspoons of baking powder
1 teaspoon of salt

Directions:

In a medium sized mixing bowl combine salt, baking powder and flour. Set aside.

In a large mixing bowl cream together sugar and butter until light and fluffy. Beat in egg, banana extract and vanilla extract. Gradually add the dry mixture to the wet mixture.

Refrigerate the cookie dough for a minimum of two hours. If desired, you can prepare the cookie dough and allow it to chill *in the refrigerator overnight.*

Preheat oven to 350 degrees.

Knead the chilled cookie dough until it becomes pliable. Dust the ¼ cup of flour onto a clean, dry surface. Using a rolling pin, roll the cookie dough out until it is ¼ of an inch in thickness.

Use cookie cutters to cut the cookies into your desired shapes. Place an 1 inch apart on the prepared cookie sheet.

Bake 8 - 10 ***minutes in the preheated oven***. If you are using icing, candies or other products to decorate, let the cookies completely cool before beginning.

# Mint Chocolate Cut Out Cookies

Ingredients:

1 cup of butter, softened

1 cup of sugar

1 egg

1 ½ teaspoons of vanilla extract

1 teaspoon of peppermint extract

2 cups of flour

½ cup of unsweetened baking cocoa

1 teaspoon of baking soda

½ teaspoon of salt

Directions:

In a medium sized mixing bowl combine the baking soda, salt, flour and cocoa. Set aside.

In a large mixing bowl, cream together the sugar and the butter until light and fluffy. Mix in the egg, peppermint extract and vanilla extract.

Gradually add the dry ingredients to the wet ingredients until well combined.

Refrigerate the cookie dough for a minimum of two hours. If desired, you can prepare the cookie dough and allow it to chill *in the refrigerator overnight.*

Preheat oven to 350 degrees.

Knead the chilled cookie dough until it becomes pliable. Dust the ¼ cup of flour onto a clean, dry surface. Using a rolling pin, roll the cookie dough out until it is ¼ of an inch in thickness.

Use cookie cutters to cut the cookies into your desired shapes. Place an 1 inch apart on the prepared cookie sheet.

Bake 8 - 10 *minutes in the preheated oven*. If you are using icing, candies or other products to decorate, let the cookies completely cool before beginning.

# Cranberry Cut Out Sugar Cookies

Ingredients:

1 ½ cups of butter, softened
2 cups of sugar
3 eggs
1 ½ teaspoons of vanilla extract
1 teaspoon of orange zest
4 ½ cups of flour
2 teaspoons of baking powder
1 teaspoon of salt
1 cup of dried cranberries

Directions:

In a medium sized mixing bowl combine the flour, baking powder and salt. Set aside.

In a large mixing bowl cream together the sugar and the butter. Beat in the eggs one at a time. Mix in the vanilla extract and orange zest.

Gradually add the dry ingredients to the wet ingredients until well combined. Fold in the cranberries.

Refrigerate the cookie dough for a minimum of two hours. If desired, you can prepare the cookie dough and allow it to chill in the refrigerator overnight.

Preheat oven to 350 degrees.

Knead the chilled cookie dough until it becomes pliable. Dust the ¼ cup of flour onto a clean, dry surface. Using a rolling pin, roll the cookie dough out until it is ¼ of an inch in thickness.

Use cookie cutters to cut the cookies into your desired shapes. Place an 1 inch apart on the prepared cookie sheet.

Bake 8 - 10 minutes in the preheated oven. If you are using icing, candies or other products to decorate, let the cookies completely cool before beginning.

# Eggnog Cut Out Cookies

Ingredients:

2 cups of sugar
1 cup of butter, softened
2 eggs
½ cup of eggnog
1 ½ teaspoons of vanilla extract
4 cups of flour
1 teaspoon of nutmeg
½ teaspoon of cinnamon
2 teaspoons of baking powder

Directions:

In a medium sized mixing bowl combine the flour, baking powder, nutmeg and cinnamon. Set aside.
In a large mixing bowl, cream together the butter and sugar until light and fluffy. Mix in the eggs one at a time. Stir in the vanilla extract and the eggnog.
Gradually add the dry mixture to the wet mixture until well combined.
Refrigerate the cookie dough for a minimum of two hours. If desired, you can prepare the cookie dough and allow it to chill *in the refrigerator overnight.*
Preheat oven to 350 degrees.

Knead the chilled cookie dough until it becomes pliable. Dust the ¼ cup of flour onto a clean, dry surface. Using a rolling pin, roll the cookie dough out until it is ¼ of an inch in thickness.

Use cookie cutters to cut the cookies into your desired shapes. Place an 1 inch apart on the prepared cookie sheet.

Bake 7-***10 minutes in the preheated oven***. If you are using icing, candies or other products to decorate, let the cookies completely cool before beginning.

# Cinnamon Mint Cut Out Cookies

Ingredients:

1 cup of butter, softened

1 cup of sugar

1 cup of powdered sugar

1 cup of vegetable oil

2 eggs

2 teaspoons of vanilla extract

1 ½ teaspoons of peppermint extract

4 ½ cups of flour

1 teaspoon of salt

1 teaspoon of baking soda

1 teaspoon of cream of tartar

1 ½ teaspoons of cinnamon, ground

Directions:

In a medium bowl combine the flour, salt, baking soda, cream of tartar and cinnamon. Set aside.

In a large mixing bowl cream together the powdered sugar, white sugar, oil and butter. Add the eggs, vanilla extract and peppermint extract.

Gradually add the dry mixture to the wet mixture until well combined.

Refrigerate the cookie dough for a minimum of two hours. If desired, you can prepare the cookie dough and allow it to chill *in the refrigerator overnight.*

Preheat oven to 375 degrees.

Knead the chilled cookie dough until it becomes pliable. Dust the ¼ cup of flour onto a clean, dry surface. Using a rolling pin, roll the cookie dough out until it is ¼ of an inch in thickness.

Use cookie cutters to cut the cookies into your desired shapes. Place an 1 inch apart on the prepared cookie sheet.

Bake 10 - 12 **minutes in the preheated oven**. If you are using icing, candies or other products to decorate, let the cookies completely cool before beginning.

# Red Velvet Cut Out Cookies

Ingredients:

1 cup of butter, softened
2 cups of powdered sugar
1 egg
2 teaspoons of vanilla extract
1 tablespoon of red velvet emulsion
3 tablespoons of milk
½ cup of cocoa powder
¼ cup of buttermilk powder
3 ½ cups of flour
2 teaspoons of baking powder
1 teaspoon of salt

Directions:

In a medium sized mixing bowl combine the salt, baking powder, cocoa, buttermilk powder and flour. Set aside.

In a large mixing bowl cream together the sugar and butter. Mix in the egg, milk, red velvet emulsion and vanilla. Mix well.

Gradually add the dry ingredients to the wet ingredients.

Refrigerate the cookie dough for a minimum of two hours. If desired, you can prepare the cookie dough and allow it to chill *in the refrigerator overnight.*

Preheat oven to 350 degrees.

Knead the chilled cookie dough until it becomes pliable. Dust the ¼ cup of flour onto a clean, dry surface. Using a rolling pin, roll the cookie dough out until it is ¼ of an inch in thickness.

Use cookie cutters to cut the cookies into your desired shapes. Place an 1 inch apart on the prepared cookie sheet.

Bake 7-***9 minutes in the preheated oven***. If you are using icing, candies or other products to decorate, let the cookies completely cool before beginning.

# Mocha Cut Out Cookies

Ingredients:

½ cup of butter, softened
½ cup of brown sugar
2 teaspoons of espresso powder
2 teaspoons of cocoa powder
½ teaspoon of salt
1 egg yolk
1 teablespoon of coffee liqueur
1 ½ cups of flour

Directions:

In a large mixing bowl, cream together brown sugar and butter. Add egg yolk and coffee liqueur.

Gradually add espresso powder, cocoa powder, salt and flour to wet mixture.

Refrigerate the cookie dough for a minimum of two hours. If desired, you can prepare the cookie dough and allow it to chill *in the refrigerator overnight.*

Preheat oven to 350 degrees.

Knead the chilled cookie dough until it becomes pliable. Dust the ¼ cup of flour onto a clean, dry surface. Using a rolling pin, roll the cookie dough out until it is ¼ of an inch in thickness.

Use cookie cutters to cut the cookies into your desired shapes. Place an 1 inch apart on the prepared cookie sheet.

Bake 11 - 13 ***minutes in the preheated oven***. If you are using icing, candies or other products to decorate, let the cookies completely cool before beginning.

# Chocolate Peanut Butter Cut Out Cookies

Ingredients:

5 cups of flour
1 cup of baking cocoa
3 teaspoons of baking powder
½ teaspoon of salt
2 cups of butter
1 cup of smooth peanut butter
2 eggs
2 ½ teaspoons of vanilla extract

Directions:

In a medium sized bowl combine the salt, baking powder, flour and cocoa. Set aside.

In a large mixing bowl beat together the sugar and butter until light and fluffy. Beat in the peanut butter. Add the egg and vanilla extract.

Gradually add the dry ingredients to the wet ingredients until well combined.

Refrigerate the cookie dough for a minimum of two hours. If desired, you can prepare the cookie dough and allow it to chill ***in the refrigerator overnight.***

Preheat oven to 350 degrees.

Knead the chilled cookie dough until it becomes pliable. Dust the ¼ cup of flour onto a clean, dry surface. Using a rolling pin, roll the cookie dough out until it is ¼ of an inch in thickness.

Use cookie cutters to cut the cookies into your desired shapes. Place an 1 inch apart on the prepared cookie sheet.

Bake 10 - 12 ***minutes in the preheated oven***. If you are using icing, candies or other products to decorate, let the cookies completely cool before beginning.

# Toffee Cut Out Cookies

Ingredients:

1 cups of butter
1 ½ cups of powdered sugar
1 egg
2 teaspoons of toffee extract
1 teaspoon of vanilla extract
3 cups of flour
1 ½ teaspoons of baking powder
1teaspoon of salt

Directions:

In a medium sized mixing bowl blend together salt, baking powder and flour. Set aside.
In a large mixing bowl cream together the sugar and the butter. Mix in the egg, toffee extract and vanilla extract.
Gradually add the dry mixture to the wet mixture.

Refrigerate the cookie dough for a minimum of two hours. If desired, you can prepare the cookie dough and allow it to chill *in the refrigerator overnight.*

Preheat oven to 350 degrees.

Knead the chilled cookie dough until it becomes pliable. Dust the ¼ cup of flour onto a clean, dry surface. Using a rolling pin, roll the cookie dough out until it is ¼ of an inch in thickness.

Use cookie cutters to cut the cookies into your desired shapes. Place an 1 inch apart on the prepared cookie sheet.

Bake 8 - 10 *minutes in the preheated oven*. If you are using icing, candies or other products to decorate, let the cookies completely cool before beginning.

## Chocolate Caramel Cut Out Cookies

Ingredients:

2 cups of flour
1 cup of cocoa powder
1 teaspoon of salt
1 cup of brown sugar
¾ cup of butter
½ cup of almond past
1 tablespoon of milk
1 teaspoon of almond extract

Directions:

In a large mixing bowl cream together sugar and butter. Add milk, almond extract and almond paste.

Gradually mix in flour, cocoa powder and salt.

Refrigerate the cookie dough for a minimum of two hours. If desired, you can prepare the cookie dough and allow it to chill *in the refrigerator overnight.*

Preheat oven to 350 degrees.

Knead the chilled cookie dough until it becomes pliable. Dust the ¼ cup of flour onto a clean, dry surface. Using a rolling pin, roll the cookie dough out until it is ¼ of an inch in thickness.

Use cookie cutters to cut the cookies into your desired shapes. Place an 1 inch apart on the prepared cookie sheet.

Bake 8 - 10 *minutes in the preheated oven*. If you are using icing, candies or other products to decorate, let the cookies completely cool before beginning.

www.ingramcontent.com/pod-product-compliance
Lightning Source LLC
Chambersburg PA
CBHW071439070526
44578CB00001B/148